Management Cases

Revised Edition

Management Cases

Revised Edition

Peter F. Drucker

Revised and Updated by
Joseph A. Maciariello

COLLINS BUSINESS
An Imprint of HarperCollins Publishers

MANAGEMENT CASES. Copyright © 1977 by Peter F. Drucker. MANAGEMENT CASES, REVISED EDITION. Copyright © 2009 by the Peter F. Drucker Literary Trust. Foreword copyright © 2009 by Warren G. Bennis. All rights reserved. Printed in the United States of America. No part of this book may be used or reproduced in any manner whatsoever without written permission except in the case of brief quotations embodied in critical articles and reviews. For information, address HarperCollins Publishers, 195 Broadway, New York, NY 10007.

HarperCollins books may be purchased for educational, business, or sales promotional use. For information, please e-mail the Special Markets Department at SPsales@harpercollins.com.

First Harper & Row edition published 1977.
First Collins Business edition published 2009.

Designed by Level C

Library of Congress Cataloging-in-Publication Data

Drucker, Peter F. (Peter Ferdinand), 1909–2005.
  Management cases / Peter F. Drucker.—Rev. ed.
      p. cm.
    ISBN 978-0-06-143515-7
  1. Industrial management—United States—Case studies. 2. Management—Case studies. I. Title.

HD70.U5D69   2008
658—dc22   2008020098

19 OV/LSC 11

Contents

Preface

The fifty cases in this book all deal with specific situations, specific problems, specific decisions—every one of them typical and fairly common in business and public service organizations. They are all management situations, management problems, and management decisions—and that means that they deal with what people have to face, what people have to resolve, and what people have to decide. They are thus typical of the kind of situation, problem, and decision everyone in management commonly faces—the kind of situations, problems, and decisions today's executives and students are likely to face tomorrow. They should thus be approached by students and instructors as cases that ask, How should one handle this?

The cases are organized into ten groups following the organization of the text *Management: Revised Edition*. They are:

    I Management's New Realities

   II Business Performance

  III Performance in Service Institutions

  IV Productive Work and Achieving Worker

   V Social Impacts and Social Responsibilities

  VI The Manager's Work and Jobs

 VII Managerial Skills

VIII Innovation and Entrepreneurship

  IX Managerial Organization

   X New Demands on the Individual

Each case has one primary focus. Each is also concerned—as is every managerial situation, managerial problem, and managerial decision—with both the organization and the whole person. Each can be read, discussed, and used for one main point and purpose; and each can be read, discussed, and used to gain insight into the complexity of institutions and of human behavior in institutions.

The cases all deal with real people in real situations and can be used in discussion groups as well as for a topic for a paper. Most important, the cases can be used to help readers convert the information and examples in the text into the real knowledge that one gains when the discipline of management is put into practice.

Peter F. Drucker

Foreword

Rigor and Relevance

The truth is that nobody can replace Peter. He was one of a kind. That's what makes a genius, that unique quality, the *sui generis,* the kind of mastery that comes once in a while and makes us feel really blessed. The beauty, for those of us who are trying to follow in his footsteps, is that, as Isaac Newton once said, "We dwarfs have the good fortune of being able to stand on the shoulders of giants which allows us to see further."

My relationship with Peter goes way back. I was first introduced to him by my main mentor, Douglas McGregor. He brought us together when I had just got out of my PhD program at MIT, and we became friends. In fact, when I first moved out to Southern California in 1980, Peter and his wife, Doris, were settled in Claremont. Shortly after I arrived in California, Peter called and invited me to have dinner. I spent the afternoon by the pool and had dinner with the Druckers.

My relationship with Peter was always interesting because I felt I was his brother. I felt he was my older brother by about two decades or so . . . and I kept seeking his approval, which I never felt I got fully. It was always so wonderful because, though he would try to do it politely, he was so straightforward. He would simply say, "Uhmm . . . but, Warren . . . you have it wrong." Peter always kept me on edge.

I want to frame this book, *Management Cases*, in terms of, "Where is business education?" I think we are going through an incredibly interesting period of looking at what it means to be business educators, especially at the MBA level. Lots of writing and controversy has been going on. Most of it is not really related. Think about the success of business education: it has grown 124 percent in the last five years alone. Of course, the growth doesn't mean everything. But, in 1959, when MIT started its first PhD program in business education, the famous Ford Foundation Report was published, and it changed what was going on in business schools. It changed business schools because not only did the Ford Foundation write a report, it also provided a lot of money to start business schools.

I have a long background in business education. There has always been this tension between rigor and relevance. Every professional school, whether it's a law school, business school, or medical school, deals with the tension between practitioners and researchers—a tension that could be so creative and constructive.

It is an old issue. I remember when I was just beginning my career, back in the late 1950s and early 1960s, there was (and still is) a very famous professor of management at Harvard Business School named Howard Raiffa who was also a mathematician and statistician. He was a very hot commodity at that time and received lots of offers. His research area is in decision-making models, and he is famous for the Raiffa Decision Model. One day, he received a very attractive offer from Stanford and he went to the dean of Harvard Business School and said, "I got this great offer from Stanford and I can't make up my mind." The dean, George Baker, replied, "Howard, why don't you apply one of your models to yourself?" Howard responded, "Yeah, but this is important!" This tension between rigor and relevance in academia is a very real problem, as this anecdote illustrates.

Peter's *Management: Tasks, Responsibilities, Practices* achieved the rigor of management education while addressing the question of relevance. This newly edited version of *Management Cases* complements the new revision of the former management book in that it reinforces relevance to rigor. In their revised form, these two great management books, *Management, Revised Edition,* and *Management Cases*, resolve this tension between rigor and relevance for students and executives of the twenty-first century.

Warren G. Bennis
Los Angeles, CA
February, 2008

Part I

Management's New Realities

Case Number 1

Yuhan-Kimberly's New Paradigm: Respect for Human Dignity*

The human resource consulting company Hewitt Associates, sponsored by *The Wall Street Journal Asia,* ranked Yuhan-Kimberly among the top ten companies on their list "Best Employers in Asia" in 2003. Mr. Seung-woo Son, the manager of public relations at Yuhan-Kimberly, attributes the foundation for such success to the corporate culture of Yuhan-Kimberly (Y-K).

The corporate culture of Y-K, in turn, is derived from the business philosophy of the company founder, Dr. Il-han New. Its five business principles are "respect for humans," "customer satisfaction," "social responsibility," "value creation," and "innovation orientation."

This case traces the impact of Y-K's first principle, "respect for humans," upon company success. In few words, the first principle implies that Y-K does not consider employees as raw materials for production (i.e., as a business cost), but considers employees as family members who can all grow together.

---

* This case was prepared by Min S. Shin of the Peter F. Drucker and Masatoshi Ito Graduate School of Management under the supervision of Professor Joseph A. Maciariello. Source material was provided by Mr. Kook-Hyun Moon, President and Chief Executive Officer of Yuhan-Kimberly, Limited, January 2008.

The "four crew/two shift system" and "lifelong learning paradigm" at Y-K is a result of the application of the first business principle. And Y-K believes that this principle is directly related to its high productivity, as shown in figure 1.1.

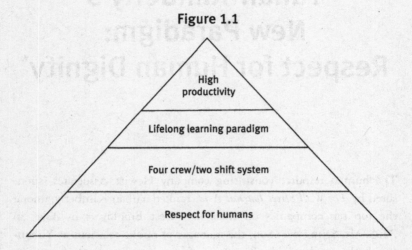

Figure 1.1

"Respect for humans" pyramid

Most observers agree that the economic success of Y-K can be partially explained by its application of its foundation principle: "respect for humans."

Kook-Hyun Moon, the former CEO and president of Y-K, is emphatic in his belief that organizational restructurings and large layoffs are *old* and unproductive *practices*. He argues that most leaders in the current business environment do not understand that the *new practice* of investing in employee development is the most beneficial one that an organization can adopt.

FOUR CREW/TWO SHIFT SYSTEM

One of the events that led to an application of Y-K's "respect for the individual" principle was its need to shut down some of its production lines for more than six months during the Asian economic crisis of the late 1990s (approximately 1997–1999).

Operating time at Y-K's manufacturing plants was reduced by more than 50 percent during this period. Organizational restructuring seemed to be Y-K's only solution. But talk of restructuring created tension between labor and management.

"Redundant employees" comprised approximately 40 percent of the total labor force. For most businesses, this excess-labor percentage would mean a large number of layoffs. However, Mr. Moon came up with an innovative solution to the problem.

Instead of a large layoff, Mr. Moon suggested a job-sharing system, a system that came to be known as the "four crew/two shift system." The system could have led to even greater financial difficulties because its implementation actually increased its labor costs. However, Mr. Moon believed that application of Y-K's human principle and the decision not to lay off Y-K's employees would overcome increased costs.

In the beginning, employees were opposed to the new system because they feared reduced wages as a result of decreased overtime pay. However, employees started to accept the new system as the Asian economic crisis worsened.

Under the system, a team works the day shift for four days, from 7:00 AM to 7:00 PM and another team works the night shift for four days, from 7:00 PM to 7:00 AM. After four days, another set of two teams takes over the two shifts and the previous two teams have four days off (3 days of rest and 1 day of paid training).

Figure 1.2

	Mon	Tue	Wed	Thu	Fri	Sat	Sun	Mon	Tue	Wed	Thu	Fri	Sat	Sun
Team A	Day shift	Day shift	Day shift	Day shift	Train	Off	Off	Off	Night shift	Night shift	Night shift	Night shift	Off	Off
Team B	Off	Off	Off	Train	Day shift	Day shift	Day shift	Day shift	Off	Off	Off	Off	Night shift	Night shift
Team C	Night shift	Night shift	Night shift	Night shift	Off	Off	Off	Train	Day shift	Day shift	Day shift	Day shift	Off	Off
Team D	Train	Off	Off	Off	Night shift	Night shift	Night shift	Night shift	Off	Off	Off	Train	Day shift	Day shift

Four crew/two shift system schedule

Figure 1.3

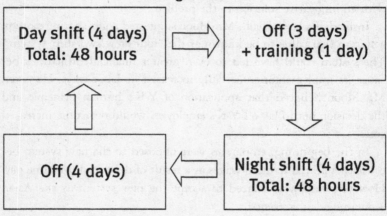

16 workday cycle

The "four crew/two shift system" started to show positive results almost immediately. A dramatic leap in productivity was realized by these employees, who now were able to take long enough rest periods to achieve full recovery and then had enough time for continuous training and education, all without Y-K ever having to halt production lines.

As a result of the system, fiscal revenue more than doubled, from

U.S. $332 million in 1996 to U.S. $704 million in 2003. Also, net income increased sixfold, from U.S. $14.4 million to U.S. $90.4 million, during the same period. But, initially job sharing reduced individual working hours by 150 hours per year and individual salaries and wages by 6 percent.

LIFELONG LEARNING—PARADIGM SHIFT

Y-K offered employees corporate-sponsored in-house educational opportunities in areas such as beginning and advanced computer skills, foreign languages, and job-related skills. Y-K also encouraged employees to further their education outside the workplace and the company agreed to support 70 percent of the cost. The implementation of the new system brought about a "life-long learning paradigm" among employees. Mr. Moon strongly believes in the importance of continuous learning to transform manual workers into knowledge workers. These workers in turn generate more ideas and are able to make more decisions on their own.

In the year immediately following implementation of the system and paradigm shift, the annual number of suggestions for improvements and innovations from workers increased by 1,200.

Beginning in the second year, the new paradigm resulted in higher productivity and higher incentive pay for individual workers. As a result, salaries and wages rose over what workers had been paid prior to the inauguration of the system. With such impressive results this innovative system was recognized as a success, because it not only increased employment but also increased the productivity and knowledge base of workers.

QUESTIONS

What in human nature accounts for the success of the Y-K rotation system? If the Y-K system is so productive and profitable, why isn't it more widely used? What would prevent such a system from being implemented in a company with which you are familiar?

Part II

Business Performance

Case Number 2

What Is OUR Business?

For as long as Bill Callahan could remember, he had always worked—indeed lived—in a retail store. His father had owned a small meat market in South Philadelphia, and young Bill had played there as a toddler and gone to work there as soon as he was old enough to hold a broom. He had worked in the market on weekends while going to school and college; and when he went into the army, he found himself almost immediately running a Post Exchange. And Bill loved every minute of it—indeed, his idea of heaven was a huge supermarket in which all the cash registers rang all the time.

Bill had known since he was eight or nine that he would own and build a retail chain—and he started on this goal the day he was discharged from the army in the mid-1960s. But he also knew that his chain would be quite different from any other. For Bill had deep convictions as to what makes a successful retail business. "No retailer can carry better or even different goods," he argued. "What he can do is first make shopping more enjoyable, friendlier, and more fun; and secondly, make the retail store a place where people like to work and a place the employees consider their own personal concern." This, according to Bill Callahan, meant three things: First, no chain could contain more than a handful of stores—no more than what one owner-manager could manage by example, by frequent visits of inspection, and by personal control. Second, each store had to have a center of strength, something that made it distinguished. And finally, the key people in each store—the manager and the department managers—had to have a personal stake in the store's success. Callahan's first store was a medium-sized supermarket on the outskirts of a metropolitan community; he got a very cheap rental, as the former operator had gone bankrupt. Within three months, Callahan's store was flourishing. "All I did," said Callahan, "was to think through the areas in which a supermarket needs excellence—its meats and produce—for everything else is packaged by the manufacturer. So I personally ran the meat and the produce departments, until they were outstanding. Then I thought through how to give distinction to a small store—and I started the first flower-and-plant department in a supermarket in my area. This completely changed the store's physical appearance and attraction, and the department also makes a good deal of money. Finally, I knew why people come back to a store—they like the way they're treated. So I stressed being friendly, being friendly, being friendly, until every employee got the idea." Nine months after the first store opened, Callahan opened the second. He moved over to the new store as manager and gave his successor at the first store a substantial share in the store's profits, with smaller shares for the department managers—all the way down to the women at the checkout counters. Within three years, Callahan had eleven stores in the same metropolitan area.

Then, instead of opening more supermarkets, he decided to start a new chain—a chain of garden centers. He repeated the pattern there—and then shifted to home-service centers for the do-it-yourself home owner, built around hand tools and small power tools. His next venture was a chain of greeting-card stores—small, high-turnover, and run by one person. Thirty years after he had started with his first store, Bill Callahan incorporated as Callahan Associates, with four chains, a total of forty stores, and in excess of $150 million in sales. Each of the chains had its own general manager who had started out as a checker or clerk and worked his or her way up through store management. Together with Callahan, a financial executive, and a human resource executive—all former store managers who had started at the bottom—they constituted the company's executive committee. The general managers of the chains had a small profit participation in Callahan Associates and a substantial participation in the profits of their own chain. Each store manager under them had a smaller share in the chain's profits and a substantial share in his or her store's profits—and so on, all the way down, with every employee with more than eighteen months of service participating in some sort of profit-sharing plan.

Callahan deeply believed that the company had to expand to give people promotional opportunities. And since he also believed that no one chain should grow beyond the point where one person could easily manage it and know every nook and cranny of it, this meant going purposefully into new businesses every six or seven years. Accordingly, he started in the fall of 1995—almost exactly thirty years after he opened his first store—to look around for the next business to go into. He finally picked two as most promising: a chain of "outdoor-wear stores"—blue jeans, boots, Western shirts, and so on; and a chain of simple restaurants featuring steak, roast beef, chicken, and so on. However, he knew that he should tackle only one of these at a time. Callahan had learned how difficult it is to get a new venture going and knew that he himself would have to spend most of his time on it for the first two or three years.

It was the policy of Callahan Associates to make all major decisions unanimously in the Executive Committee. In the past that had been very much a formality—the members followed Callahan's lead. But when he brought up the new expansion plans, Callahan unexpectedly ran into serious opposition. Everyone agreed that it was time to get a new venture going. Everyone agreed that they had to concentrate on one venture. Indeed, everyone seemed to agree that the two areas Callahan had picked offered excellent opportunities. But half the group was bitterly opposed to going into anything that had to do with "fashion" (the outdoor-wear business), and the other half was as bitterly opposed to going into a "personal service" business (restaurants).

"We know a good deal about food and home products," said the first group. "Our customers are housewives and home owners. 'Outdoor wear'—that's kids to begin with, and it is style and promotion and sex appeal—not our bag." "Restaurants," the others argued, "are not for us. We know how to sell things to people, but restaurants sell service and atmosphere and have to cook and cater to guests—not our bag."

"All right," said a thoroughly exasperated Callahan, "you have told me what our business is NOT—but how does one go about deciding what it is or should be? You all agree that the market opportunities are good in both areas. So what we need to think through is what it is *we* are, *we* can do, *we* believe in."

QUESTION

How could one go about thinking through these questions?

Case Number 3

What Is a Growth Company?

An old established baker of bread and cakes, distributed widely in one of the country's major metropolitan areas, was bought by a large, publicly traded, private-equity firm. The bakery's stock was selling at eight times earnings on the stock market; the private-equity firm had offered fourteen times earnings, an irresistible offer. It paid with its own stock, which then sold at twenty-two times earnings—so everybody was happy or should have been. The president of the bakery—a middle-aged but very vigorous member of the founding family, in fact, a grandson of the Swedish immigrant who had started the business around 1890—agreed to stay on with a five-year contract.

Six months after the acquisition had been consummated, the bakery's president was called to New York headquarters for a meeting with the corporate president. "You know, John," the president said, "that it is our policy that each of our divisions show 10 percent growth a year and make a return of at least 15 percent pretax on investment. Your division is growing only at 1 or 2 percent a year and shows only 7 percent pretax—no more than we can get in a savings-bank account. Our staff people are ready to sit down with you and turn your business around so that it can meet our growth and profit objectives."

"I am afraid," answered the bakery's president, "that they would be wasting their time, and mine. A bakery is not a growth business, and nothing you do can make it into one. People don't eat more bread, or even more cakes; as their incomes go up, they eat less. A bakery has built-in protection against a downturn; in fact, we'd probably do best in a really serious depression. But our growth isn't going to be faster than that of population. And as for profits, we get paid for being efficient. I know we need to be far more efficient, but that would require fairly massive investment in new automated bakeries, and with our price-earnings ratio, we have never felt able to raise the kind of money we need. Even if we did automate, our rate of return isn't going to be more than 12 percent pretax at best."

"This is unacceptable," snapped the president. "I agree," said the bakery man. "Indeed, this is precisely the reason we gladly accepted your offer to buy us out: we had to free our family's own money for more attractive investments, and all our money was in the bakery. That's also the reason why all of us immediately sold your company's stock. And that's the reason that I am quite willing for you to buy up my employment contract. If you want to run a bread bakery as a growth company, you'd better buy me out—I wouldn't know how to try."

QUESTIONS

Can one be satisfied with a business that earns less than the minimum cost of capital and cannot raise the capital it needs to become efficient? If not, what (if anything) can be done? And who is right?: the man who says that this kind of business cannot be run at a 15 percent profit level, or the man who says that if the market is there, it is management's job to earn a return that can attract the needed capital? Are both wrong? Or could both be right?

Case Number 4

Success in the Small Multinational

It is commonly believed that multinational corporations have to be very large. Indeed, a fairly popular criterion defines multinationals as companies that have at least $200 million in sales. But actually, there are a great many small companies that have been outstandingly successful, if only because they are politically so much less visible.

A good example of the small and highly successful multinational company is a small Swiss company, Urania A.G., located in the small town—hardly more than a village—of Glarus in eastern Switzerland. The company's history is a very peculiar one: in the late 1960s, Urania was on the point of liquidation, totally unsuccessful and, indeed, practically bankrupt.

The story actually begins with a man, Christian Bluntschli, now in his nineties. Bluntschli, who had been educated as an engineer in Zurich, came in the early 1930s to Philadelphia's Wharton School as an exchange student. He stayed long enough to get a master's degree and then a doctorate. When he went back to Switzerland, he was promptly hired by that country's first business school, the Commercial University in St. Gallen. He became a very successful and popular professor of finance and stayed until the late 1960s. Then he went to one of the big Swiss banks as an economist. But he found himself rather bored by the work. When the Wharton School approached him with the suggestion that he come to Philadelphia and join the faculty, he was on the point of accepting.

But before he could resign, the bank's president called him in and said, "I wonder, Bluntschli, whether you would take on a special assignment? We have lent a lot of money to a small company which makes precision gears in Glarus, Urania A.G. We now own about 35 percent of the stock. The company seems to be in terrible trouble; in fact, I strongly suspect that it is completely bankrupt. It seems we should liquidate, but the company is the largest employer in a poor rural area, and we are rather worried about the public relations aspect of letting it go out of business. Could you go down to Glarus and look into the affairs of the company and tell us whether you think that salvage is worth trying?"

When Bluntschli went to Glarus, he found the situation much worse than anything he had been prepared for. Early in the twentieth century, the company had been the world's leading supplier of gears for the then-fashionable cog railways. But cog railways had gone out of fashion, replaced by cable cars and rope tows. And although the company had the right products needed for the manufacture of these replacements, it had never tried to sell them. Instead, it had built tremendous service staffs and spare-part inventories to service old cog-railway customers everywhere. In Japan alone it had twenty-eight trained people on its payroll to supply spare parts and service to only twelve customers—all of them themselves losing money and going out of business. The people who ran the company had spent all of their time and the company's money on a wide variety of fields. However, they had never done anything with their patents. Their policy was not to license but to manufacture. Where they could not manufacture—and in few of the areas in which they had taken out patents did they have any manufacturing capability—they simply did nothing.

The more Bluntschli saw, the more depressed he became. But also he was excited by the worldwide service capability the company had built up. Finally—he himself says, "in a fit of temporary insanity"—

he decided that managing Urania was what he wanted to do. He went to his associates in the bank and said, "The company is hopeless. How much do I have to pay you for its ownership?" And before he could recover from his temporary insanity, he owned 100 percent of a bankrupt company with no business, no working capital, and no assets, except for an excellent worldwide service staff.

That was in the 1960s. Today, Urania is one of the most profitable small businesses in the world. It still employs only about nine hundred people. But it is the leader in precision gearing—in specialized transportation such as cable cars, ski tows, mining gondolas, and in the special gearing needed for the equipment to put containers on ships and so on. It actually has manufacturing facilities in about thirty countries, but it makes only one or two parts of each of the patented pieces of equipment it sells. Whatever is standard is contracted out to be made on the spot. It still focuses on service, and especially on design service. But it now charges for service and makes enough profit on service to cover its entire worldwide payroll. Whatever it gets for selling equipment, minus what it has to pay to its own suppliers, is, in effect, net profit.

When you ask Bluntschli how he got there, he smiles and says, "I did only the obvious things, the things you find in each textbook."

QUESTION

What do you think Bluntschli did that neither his predecessors in the ownership and management of Urania nor his associates in the bank did?

Case Number 5

Health Care as a Business

One of the country's leading manufacturers, a company with a long record of leadership in advanced technology, decided around 1985 that major future growth would be in community services, rather than in traditional "hardware," in which the company has always specialized. One of the fields identified as a major growth area was health care. And so a task force was set up to study the hospital, its management, needs, and direction. The assignment was first to look inside the hospital—not to ask what business opportunities it might offer. Only after the task force had decided what the hospital itself should or might be was it expected to concern itself with health care as a business opportunity.

After a year's study, the task force decided that the best way to learn about the hospital was to go into hospital consulting. Accordingly, a small staff was set up to do hospital consulting. It soon became the leading hospital consultant in the country, doing a large number of assignments for all kinds of hospitals—and, apparently, doing them well.

At the same time, work was continued on the study and design of the "ideal hospital." After the hospital consulting activity had already established itself as highly successful and profitable, the task force people went back to top management and said: "There is no doubt in our minds that the hospital needs major restructuring. In fact we know what is wrong with the hospital and what it needs. We can design a hospital which will give better patient care more economically. It would be a very different hospital from any that is around now. But we think that within a few years the country will be ready to consider major innovations in the hospital; we are clearly moving toward a grave crisis of confidence in the present health-care system.

"There are three possible approaches. We can design the hardware for tomorrow's hospital, which will need an incredible amount of advanced technology. This is fully within the competence of this company. It would also be fully in line with the company's tradition. It has always been a manufacturer of advanced equipment for a large variety of industrial and institutional users. It could be the company that has the best and most advanced hospital equipment and at the same time knows what to do with it."

"The second approach is to be hospital designers and hospital builders. We could do what GE and Westinghouse did in the nuclear reactor field and build—whether for the government or the Board of a community hospital—a complete hospital that we can then turn over to them to run. And—perhaps even more successfully—we could remodel old and inefficient hospitals—that is, practically all the hospitals in existence today.

"Finally, we could go into the hospital business. Hospital bills are more and more being paid by 'third-party interests'—the government, HMOs, Blue Cross, and insurance carriers. Hospital operating expenses, in other words, are being underwritten. And so are the costs of capital in hospitals. This is, therefore, a possible business opportunity. We could take over hospitals, especially in small and medium-sized communities, where the need is great and the hospital usually quite inadequate. We could then build the right hospital and run it at a fairly substantial return on capital—and with a good captive market for our hardware."

QUESTIONS

In order to understand what each of these approaches implies, what questions does top management have to ask? What kinds of considerations apply? What facts, figures, guesses, assumptions need to be tested? What, in other words, would have to be known—or at least discussed—before top management could even address itself to the decision?

Part III

Performance in Service Institutions

Case Number 6

The University Art Museum: Defining Purpose and Mission

Visitors to the campus were always shown the University Art Museum, of which the large and distinguished university was very proud. A photograph of the handsome neoclassical building that housed the museum had long been used by the university for the cover of its brochures and catalogues.

The building, together with a substantial endowment, had been given to the university around 1932 by an alumnus, the son of the university's first president, who had become very wealthy as an investment banker. He also gave the university his own small, but high quality, collections—one of Etruscan figurines and one, unique in America, of English Pre-Raphaelite paintings. He then served as the museum's unpaid director until his death. During his tenure he brought a few additional collections to the museum, largely from other alumni of the university. Only rarely did the museum purchase anything. As a result, the museum housed several small collections of uneven quality. As long as the founder ran the museum, none of the collections were ever shown to anybody except a few members of the university's art history faculty, who were admitted as the founder's private guests.

After the founder's death, in the late 1940s, the university intended to bring in a professional museum director. Indeed, this had been part of the agreement under which the founder had given the museum. A search committee was to be appointed; but in the meantime, a graduate student in art history who had shown interest in the museum and who had spent a good many hours in it took over temporarily. At first, she did not even have a title, let alone a salary. But she stayed on acting as the museum's director and, over the next thirty years, was promoted, in stages, to that title. But from that first day, whatever her title, she had been in charge. She immediately set about changing the museum altogether. She catalogued the collections. She pursued new gifts, again primarily small collections from alumni and other friends of the university. She organized fund-raising for the museum. But, above all, Miss Kirkhoff began to integrate the museum into the work of the university. When a space problem arose, she offered the third floor of the museum to the art history faculty, which moved its offices there. She remodeled the building to include classrooms and a modern and well-appointed auditorium. She raised funds to build one of the best research-and-reference art-history libraries in the country. She also began to organize a series of special exhibitions built around the museum's own collections, complemented by loans from outside collections. For each of these exhibitions she had a distinguished member of the university's art faculty write a catalogue. These catalogues speedily became the leading scholarly texts in the fields.

Miss Kirkhoff ran the University Art Museum for almost half a century. But old age ultimately defeated her. At the age of sixty-eight, after suffering a severe stroke, she had to retire. In her letter of resignation she proudly pointed to the museum's growth and accomplishment under her stewardship. "Our endowment," she wrote, "now compares favorably with museums several times our size. We never have had to ask the university for any money other than for our share of the university's insurance policies. Our collections in the areas of our strength, while small, are of first-rate quality and importance. Above all, we are being used by more people than any museum of our size. Our lecture series, in which members of the university's art history faculty present a major subject to a university audience of students and faculty, attract regularly three to five hundred people; and if we had the seating capacity, we could easily have a larger audience. Our exhibitions are seen and studied by more visitors, most of them members of the university community, than all but the most highly publicized exhibitions in the very big museums ever draw. Above all, the courses and seminars offered in the museum have become one of the most popular and most rapidly growing educational features of the university. No other museum in this country or anywhere else," concluded Miss Kirkhoff, "has so successfully integrated art into the life of a major university and a major university into the work of a museum."

Miss Kirkhoff strongly recommended that the university bring in a professional museum director as her successor. "The museum is much too big and much too important to be entrusted to another amateur such as I was forty-five years ago," she wrote. "And it needs careful thinking regarding its direction, its basis of support, and its future relationship with the university."

The university took Miss Kirkhoff's advice. A search committee was duly appointed, and after one year's work, it produced a candidate whom everybody approved. The candidate was himself a graduate of the university who had then obtained his PhD in art history and museum work from the university. Both his teaching and administrative record were sound, leading to his present museum directorship in a medium-sized city. There he had converted an old, well-known, but rather sleepy museum into a lively, community-oriented museum whose exhibitions were well publicized and attracted large crowds.

The new museum director took over with great fanfare in September 2001. Less than three years later he left—with less fanfare, but still with considerable noise. Whether he resigned or was fired was not quite clear. But that there was bitterness on both sides was only too obvious.

The new director, upon his arrival, had announced that he looked upon the museum as a "major community resource" and intended to "make the tremendous artistic and scholarly resources of the museum fully available to the academic community as well as to the public." When he said these things in an interview with the college newspaper, everybody nodded in approval. It soon became clear that what he meant by "community resource" and what the faculty and students understood by these words were not the same. The museum had always been "open to the public," but, in practice, it was members of the college community who used the museum and attended its lectures, its exhibitions, and its frequent seminars.

The first thing the new director did, however, was to promote visits from the public schools in the area. He soon began to change the exhibition policy. Instead of organizing small shows, focused on a major collection of the museum and built around a scholarly catalogue, he began to organize "popular exhibitions" around "topics of general interest" such as "Women Artists through the Ages." He promoted these exhibitions vigorously in the newspapers, in radio and television interviews and, above all, in the local schools. As a result, what had been a busy but quiet place was soon knee-deep in school children, taken to the museum in special buses that cluttered the access roads around the museum and throughout the campus. The faculty, which was not particularly happy with the resulting noise and confusion, became thoroughly upset when the scholarly old chairman of the art history department was mobbed by fourth graders who sprayed him with their water pistols as he tried to push his way through the main hall to his office.

Increasingly, the new director did not design his own shows, but brought in traveling exhibitions from major museums, importing their catalogue, as well, rather than having his own faculty produce one.

The students, too, were apparently unenthusiastic after the first six or eight months, during which the new director had been somewhat of a campus hero. Attendance at the classes and seminars held in the art museum fell off sharply, as did attendance at the evening lectures. When the editor of the campus newspaper interviewed students for a story on the museum, he was told again and again that the museum had become too noisy and too "sensational" for students to enjoy the classes and to have a chance to learn.

What brought all this to a head was an Islamic art exhibit in late 2003. Since the museum had little Islamic art, nobody criticized the showing of a traveling exhibit, offered on very advantageous terms with generous financial assistance from some of the Arab governments. But then, instead of inviting one of the university's own faculty members to deliver the customary talk at the opening of the exhibit, the director brought in the cultural attaché of one of the Arab embassies in Washington, DC. The speaker, it was reported, used the occasion to deliver a violent attack on Israel and on the American policy of supporting Israel. A week later, the university senate decided to appoint an advisory committee, drawn mostly from members of the art history faculty, which, in the future, would have to approve all plans for exhibits and lectures. The director thereupon, in an interview with the campus newspaper, sharply attacked the faculty as "elitist" and "snobbish" and as believing that "art belongs to the rich." Six months later, in June 2004, his resignation was announced.

Under the bylaws of the university, the academic senate appoints a search committee. Normally, this is pure formality. The chairman of the appropriate department submits the department's nominees, who are approved and appointed, usually without debate. But when the academic senate, early the following semester, was asked, to appoint the search committee, things were far from "normal." The dean who presided, sensing the tempers in the room, tried to smooth over things by saying, "Clearly, we picked the wrong person the last time. We will have to try very hard this time."

He was immediately interrupted by an economist, known for his populism, who broke in and said, "I admit that the late director was probably not the right personality. But I strongly believe that the personality was not at the root of the problem. He tried to do what needs doing and that got him in trouble with the faculty. He tried to make our museum a community resource, to bring in the community and to make art accessible to broad masses of people, to the African-Americans and the Puerto Ricans, to the kids from the inner-city schools, and to the lay public. And this is what we really resented. Maybe his methods were not the most tactful ones—I admit I could have done without those interviews he gave. But what he tried to do was right. We had better commit ourselves to the policy he wanted to put into effect, or else we will have deserved his attacks on us as 'elitist' and 'snobbish.'"

"This is nonsense," cut in the usually silent and polite senate member from the art history faculty. "It makes absolutely no sense for our museum to try to become the kind of community resource our late director and my distinguished colleague want it to be. First, there is no need. The city has one of the world's finest and biggest museums and it does exactly that and does it very well. Secondly, we here have neither the artistic resources nor the financial resources to serve the community at large. We can do something different but equally important and equally unique. Ours is the only museum in the country, and perhaps in the world, that is fully integrated with the academic community and truly a teaching institution. We are using it, or at least we used to until the last few unfortunate years, as a major educational resource for all our students. No other museum in the country, and as far as I know in the world, is bringing undergraduates into art the way we do. All of us, in addition to our scholarly and graduate work, teach undergraduate courses for people who are not going to be art majors or art historians. We work with the engineering students and show them what we do in our conservation and restoration work. We work with architecture students and show them the development of architecture through the ages. Above all, we work with liberal arts students, who often have had no exposure to art before they came here and who enjoy our courses all the more because they are scholarly and not just 'art appreciation.' This is unique and this is what our museum can do and should do."

"I doubt that this is really what we should be doing," commented the chairman of the mathematics department. "The museum, as far as

I know, is part of the graduate faculty. It should concentrate on training art historians in its PhD program, on its scholarly work, and on its research. I would strongly urge that the museum be considered an adjunct to graduate and especially to PhD education, confine itself to this work, and stay out of all attempts to be 'popular,' both on campus and outside of it. The glory of the museum is the scholarly catalogues produced by our faculty, and our PhD graduates who are sought after by art history faculties throughout the country. This is the museum's mission, which can only be impaired by the attempt to be 'popular,' whether with students or with the public."

"These are very interesting and important comments," said the dean, still trying to pacify. "But I think this can wait until we know who the new director is going to be. Then we should raise these questions with him."

"I beg to differ, Mr. Dean," said one of the elder statesmen of the faculty. "During the summer months, I discussed this question with an old friend and neighbor of mine in the country, the director of one of the nation's great museums. He said to me: 'You do not have a personality problem; you have a management problem. You have not, as a university, taken responsibility for the mission, the direction, and the objectives of your museum. Until you do this, no director can succeed. And this is *your* decision. In fact, you cannot hope to get a good person until you can tell him or her what your basic objectives are. If your late director is to blame—I know him and I know that he is abrasive—it is for being willing to take on a job when you, the university, had not faced up to the basic management decisions. There is no point talking about *who* should manage until it is clear *what* it is that has to be managed and for what.'"

At this point the dean realized that he had to adjourn the discussion unless he wanted the meeting to degenerate into a brawl. But he also realized that he had to identify the issues and possible decisions before the next faculty meeting a month later. Here is the list of questions he put down on paper later that evening:

1. What are the possible purposes of the University Museum?
   ___ to serve as a laboratory for the graduate art-history faculty and the doctoral students in the field?

   ___ to serve as major "enrichment" for the undergraduate who is not an art-history student but wants both a "liberal education" and a counterweight to the highly bookish diet fed to him in most of our courses?

   ___ to serve the metropolitan community—and especially its schools—outside the campus gates?

2. Who are or should be its customers?
   ___ the graduate students in professional training to be teachers of art history?

   ___ the undergraduate community—or rather, the entire college community?

   ___ the metropolitan community and especially the teachers and youngsters in the public schools?

   ___ any others?

3. Which of these purposes are compatible and could be served simultaneously? Which are mutually exclusive or at the very least are likely to get in each other's way?

4. What implications for the structure of the museum, the qualifications of its director, and its relationship to the university follow from each of the above purposes?

5. Do we need to find out more about the needs and wants of our various potential customers to make an intelligent policy decision? How could we go about that?

The dean distributed these questions to the members of the faculty with the request that they think them through and discuss them before the next meeting of the academic senate.

QUESTIONS

How would you tackle these questions? And are they the right questions?

Case Number 7

Rural Development Institute: Should It Tackle the Problem of the Landless Poor in India?*

In October of 1999, Roy Prosterman, founder and president of the Rural Development Institute (RDI), and Tim Hanstad, RDI's executive director, spent an afternoon in a conference room debating the pros and cons of expanding RDI's operations into India. They struggled with this decision, about whether RDI should enter India, against the backdrop of RDI's long history of success. Since the early 1970s, RDI had successfully pursued its mission of alleviating poverty by securing land rights for the world's rural poor. RDI achieved its mission through four different activities: research, reform design, policy advocacy, and implementation. Arguably the most important and time-consuming of these activities was reform design, which

* Kim Jonker prepared this case, with guidance from Professor William Meehan, as the basis for class discussion, rather than as an illustration of either effective or ineffective handling of an administrative situation.

required RDI staff attorneys to live abroad and work directly with the governments of developing countries in designing programs to allocate land to rural peasants. To date, RDI had worked successfully in forty countries across the globe; it was notable that RDI had yet to establish a presence in India.

The opportunity in India was tremendous. India had the largest population of poor in the world, and there was a strong link between poverty and landlessness. However, the challenges—led by the apparent lack of political will for reform, which experience had shown was a necessary prerequisite for success—appeared to be as daunting as the opportunity was exciting. Prosterman and Hanstad weighed the opportunity against the risks.

THE RURAL DEVELOPMENT INSTITUTE
The Importance of Land Ownership for the Rural Poor

Land is the most crucial asset for the rural poor—the fundamental source of income, wealth, security, and status. Providing poor rural households with plots of land furnished recipient families with many benefits that persisted and even increased over time. These benefits included improvements in nutrition and health, income, economic security, access to credit, self-esteem, and community status. Plots of land large enough to sustain a small garden or even a few trees could increase the quantity and quality of food consumption, resulting in better overall family nutrition and health. Plots could also enhance a family's income and economic security, allowing them to produce both a surplus for sale in the market and provision for the family to fall back on in times of need. Land could even improve a family's economic position through use as collateral, which increased a family's ability to access credit either for investment or in times of distress. The self-image and community status of rural households were also enhanced by ownership of land. Such status was important for overall well-being, for its ability to increase a family's involvement in village politics, and for helping households to access informal sources of credit in the village.

The importance of land ownership in alleviating poverty among the world's poor had led to the creation of RDI.

The Origins of RDI

In 1965, Prosterman left a rising career with a top U.S. law firm, Sullivan and Cromwell, to pursue his desire to apply the law in the service of alleviating poverty. The vision that drove his early work was to provide innovative approaches to alleviating poverty and satisfying grievances through peaceful land reform. In 1967, for example, Prosterman traveled to South Vietnam to find out whether some of the underlying social and economic causes of the Vietnam War might be addressed by redistributing land to poor tenant farmers and paying reasonable compensation to landlords. Prosterman's idea caught the attention of U.S. policymakers seeking a political settlement to the conflict in Vietnam. Soon he found himself in the middle of the war, drafting legislation for a "land-to-the tiller" program—carried out by the Thieu government between 1970 and 1973—that provided land ownership to 1 million tenant farmer families, chiefly in the Mekong Delta region. Although too late to halt the conflict, the program cut Vietcong recruitment by 80 percent and boosted rice production by 30 percent.

The RDI organization and its programs grew and evolved over the years while maintaining their focus on land ownership for the rural poor. During the 1990s, for instance, in the former Communist economies, RDI focused on facilitating the voluntary breakup of collective and state farms and on establishing long-term private land rights for family farmers—including the right to buy, sell, mortgage, and pass on land by inheritance. These programs typically involved moving land from public to private ownership or equivalent long-term private tenure. Despite the continuous evolution of RDI's programs to meet the world's changing circumstances, RDI's fundamental mission had remained unchanged over the years.

RDI's Mission and Operations

According to the organization's mission statement, "RDI is a nonprofit organization of attorneys helping the rural poor in developing countries to obtain legal rights to land." The organization pursued this mission through four major activities: research, reform design, policy advocacy, and implementation. (See Exhibit 1 for RDI's mission, vision, and values statement.)

1. Research

RDI had an extensive research arm that carried out intensive interviews with the rural poor and others at village level, as well as desk research. This research was published widely. The RDI research arm disseminated findings and best practices regarding land reform and the benefits of land ownership.

2. Reform Design

RDI reviewed land reform programs and needs in forty different countries and helped design new land reform measures in many of them. This vast experience enabled RDI to become a leading source of expertise on rural land issues for a variety of international agencies, including the World Bank, the U.S. Agency for International Development (USAID), the U.N. Development Program, and the U.N. Food and Agriculture Organization.

3. Policy Advocacy

In its policy advocacy work, RDI was a driving force in pushing land rights issues to the forefront of thinking on poverty alleviation. Prosterman and his colleagues convinced leaders in many countries that practical measures to establish land ownership, or equivalent secure land rights, for the poor were an important part of economic development and the prevention of violence. This extended as well to major donor agencies in the foreign aid field. For example, because of RDI input, the U.S. government's Millennium Challenge Agency programs (a foreign aid package) recognized basic land rights for the rural poor as a fundamental item on the United States' global aid agenda.

4. Implementation

Implementation was extremely important; without effective implementation, RDI's land reform designs were not helpful to the rural poor. Nevertheless, implementation offered RDI relatively less opportunity for impact than the other three activities, because many other aid organizations and international development contractors were well qualified to do the implementation for RDI. Consequently, RDI often outsourced the implementation of its land reform designs while providing necessary guidance and oversight.

RDI's Comparative Advantage: Four Activities Combined

RDI was unique in that no other organizations that focused on land were involved in all four of the activities described above; most worked through just one or two of these approaches. A large number of organizations did research; a few undertook reform design; many did advocacy and implementation (the latter were typically international development contractors). No other organizations that focused on land were engaging in the first three activities together, much less the fourth element as well. (See Exhibit 2 for statistics on people benefiting from RDI's programs as of 1999.)

Democratic Land Reform as Advocated by RDI

RDI was extremely influential in improving perceptions of the concept of land reform and demonstrating its effectiveness throughout the world. RDI promoted democratic land reform, which stood in sharp opposition to the widely known and negatively perceived Marxist variety. Democratic land reform was carried out under the law and without violence, and it provided private landowners fair compensation for any land acquired. Democratic land reform also left land recipients free to choose how they would farm (nearly all chose to farm as family farmers, rather than in collectives or cooperatives). For example, the "land-to-the-tiller" reform carried out in South Vietnam between 1970 and 1973—on which RDI worked—paid large land-lords in the Mekong Delta in eight-year bonds worth 2.5 times gross crop value for the land redistributed to one million tenant farmers. This reform proved to be so successful that it became a major reason for the Communist government of Vietnam abandoning collective farming during the 1980s and adopting the family-farm model of the South for the whole country. As the model evolved, less of the needed land required seizure under "eminent domain": in China, for example, farmers could obtain long-term primary rights on publicly owned lands they already occupied.

THE DECISION AT HAND: SHOULD RDI EXPAND ITS OPERATIONS INTO INDIA?
The Opportunity in India

For RDI, India was particularly attractive because it was "off the charts" in meeting the two most important criteria RDI had for op-erating in a country: there was a large potential pool of beneficiaries and a close link between land and poverty. As one of the two most populous developing countries, India had the largest number of poor people on the planet in 1999. India also had the greatest concentration of rural households that were landless or nearly landless (62 million households). Furthermore, landlessness and poverty were closely linked in India. In fact, a 1997 World Bank report showed that landlessness was by far the greatest predictor of poverty in India—even more so than caste or illiteracy. For these reasons, Prosterman and Hanstad found the possibility of entering India extremely compelling. "It was the kind of opportunity that makes nonprofit leaders who aspire to make a difference absolutely starry-eyed," explained Hanstad.

The Risks and Challenges of Expanding Operations into India

Yet this "high-reward" opportunity also entailed great risk and sig-nificant challenges, and Prosterman and Hanstad wondered how those hurdles could be overcome, if at all. First and foremost was their concern about "political will." Before entering a country, RDI typically ensured that there was sufficient local political desire to pursue and implement the RDI-recommended initiatives. Hanstad explained:

> We always asked ourselves, do the political forces appear to be aligned or at least not strongly opposed? And the conventional wisdom in the 1980s and 1990s was that in India there was insufficient political will for land reform. For example, at a World Bank land policy seminar in 1999, the World Bank official in charge of rural development said, "We aren't doing anything on land in India because it is too controversial; there is no political will."

Prosterman and Hanstad believed that there were areas of potential support in the Indian political landscape that offered promise to RDI, but nevertheless they were certain that the situation would be a challenging one.

Their second concern was funding. RDI did not have any earmarked revenue for new operations in India, and Prosterman and Hanstad were unsure if they could obtain the new funding that would be necessary to achieve significant long-term impact. The uncertainty of the funding situation meant that even if Prosterman and Hanstad did decide that it made sense to enter India, it was unclear how long RDI could stay in the country. Operations in India would be particularly expensive because the various challenges inherent in Indian land reform meant that an on-the-ground office would need to be established. To date, RDI had never established an in-country office on its own with its own funds. Entering India would require RDI to obtain additional funds and/or divert existing resources away from other RDI initiatives and program areas. This was very threatening to many RDI staff members, many of whom felt that their jobs could be in jeopardy if RDI entered India.

In contrast, focusing RDI's scarce resources in other regions of the world would provide the staff with significantly more job security. For example, there was a great deal of "easy money" to be garnered in the former Soviet countries, where RDI had already developed a strong presence. RDI had established many fee-for-service opportunities in the former Soviet countries, and there were large sums of money flowing to that region of the world at the time. Hanstad observed:

> It would have been a no-brainer to forget about India and stay in the former Soviet Union except for one major factor: we had already reached a point of diminishing returns in the former Soviet Union. While we had made fantastic gains in the former Soviet Union, RDI's major value-added had already been provided. India, on the other hand, was a vast, totally untapped market full of incredible potential.

The third major challenge was that RDI would need to dramatically alter its programmatic approach in order to adapt to the Indian context. The sheer number of landless people made India distinct from all of the other countries in which RDI had been active to date. Specifically, the number of non-landowning families in India was so large that 20–40 percent of the country's land would be required in order to achieve traditional land reform, which allocated "full-size" farms of 2 to 5 acres—a more typical size for RDI, and historically elsewhere in Asia. This was, of course, impossible. The reality of these numbers meant that RDI would be forced to limit the size of the beneficiary pool, decrease the plot size per family, and/or redesign its program approach in some other as yet undetermined way. Moreover, each of the twenty-eight Indian states formulated its own land-tenure rules and reforms, so RDI would likely have to deal with a multiplicity of participants, rather than just one central decision-maker.

THE HISTORICAL CONTEXT: PREVIOUS KEY DECISIONS BY RDI

As they weighed the decision about entering India, Prosterman and Hanstad took into consideration RDI's recent history and some of its key decisions. Reflecting back on the various critical decisions that had shaped RDI's focus and effectiveness over the years, they recognized that decisions to avoid or pass up certain opportunities had been as important as decisions to actively pursue other more favorable opportunities.

RDI Stayed Focused on Mission in the Former Soviet Union

From a funding standpoint, the previous few years had been somewhat precarious for RDI, but the institute had managed to persevere while staying focused on its mission. In 1997, 70 percent of RDI's $1 million budget was earmarked for Russia and was at significant risk because the larger project under which RDI had been working in Russia was also at risk. RDI received most of that $700,000 as an annual grant from the Harvard Institute for International Development, which in turn received its funding from the U.S. Agency for International Development. There was a strong possibility that USAID's funding to Harvard would decrease significantly, which in turn meant that Harvard's funding for RDI's work in the former Soviet Union was in jeopardy.

Against this backdrop, in 1998 RDI was presented with a compelling, fully-funded opportunity that would provide a significant alternative revenue source. Another USAID contractor approached RDI to work on an urban land reform project in the former Soviet Union. This would be a new program area for RDI; to date RDI had done work only in rural settings.

The opportunity was compelling because it offered a way to diversify RDI's revenue stream and also because it built on many of the lessons that RDI had learned in previous work in Russia. RDI had developed a great deal of expertise in Russian land law through its work on rural land reform; much of this expertise and the accompanying legal framework could be applied directly to urban settings. Despite these learning economies and synergies, however, RDI would still have to devote significant time and energy on the ground to understanding the impact of urban land reform; in this respect, RDI would be starting from scratch. Prosterman and Hanstad were concerned that if they accepted the project they would lead the organization away from its niche and mission of promoting land rights for the rural poor. Hanstad explained:

> There was so much work to be done in the rural setting . . . in the end we turned down the urban opportunity because we felt that it was outside of our mission . . . and we felt very strongly that on principle we shouldn't chase after funding. It turned out to be the right decision for RDI . . . we ultimately developed a strong presence in the former Soviet Union within our niche of rural land reform . . . we obtained considerable fee-for-service opportunities, which solidified our funding and enabled us to focus directly on our mission.

RDI Passed Up Opportunities with Insufficient Scale in East Timor

RDI assessed its performance in many ways, but the metric most commonly used within the organization was simply the number of landless people receiving land rights as a result of RDI's work. RDI's "focus on the numbers" meant that scalability was always a critical factor in its decisions to enter new countries. Over the years, RDI had turned down many opportunities that were not sufficiently scalable. For example, RDI decided not to enter East Timor, which had many serious land problems, but was a very small country. "Even if we were successful in East Timor, our reach would have been small because it is such a small country . . . our efforts and resources carry great opportunity costs and so we have to focus on the places where we can have the greatest impact," explained Hanstad.

RDI Exited Kyrgyzstan upon Reaching Diminishing Returns

RDI entered Kyrgyzstan in 1992 and worked there for over seven years, achieving great success. After having significant impact, however, RDI reached a point of diminishing returns in its work. This point came after RDI completed the first three of its main activities: research, reform design, and policy advocacy. Hanstad explained:

RDI typically gets the most bang for the buck in the first three of RDI's four activities, and this is especially true in a small country. The fourth activity, implementation, is extremely important but offers RDI relatively less opportunity for impact, not least because many others are qualified to do the implementation for us. So the question at hand was whether RDI would stay in Kyrgyzstan for implementation . . . We decided to exit because there were a large number of aid agencies that were in Kyrgyzstan at the time and all of them were well qualified to oversee the ongoing implementation, which appeared to be moving forward well.

OPERATING A NONPROFIT IN THE INTERNATIONAL CONTEXT
The NGO Environment in India

When RDI was considering entering India in 1999, many other nongovernmental organizations were working in the country. Few, however, were working directly in the area of land reform, and none were working on the four paths that RDI pursued. Moreover, both the NGOs and the public entities had largely given up on the prospects for land reform measures as traditionally pursued.

The Challenges of Working with
Governments of Developing Countries:
Bureaucracy, "Red Tape," and Corruption

Hanstad and Prosterman were familiar with many of the challenges of operating a nonprofit in developing countries. Over the years, they had experienced many encounters with large bureaucracies, overwhelming "red tape," and rampant corruption. Hanstad and Prosterman knew that they would not be immune to such challenges while operating in India. In fact, Transparency International's Corruption Perceptions Index classified India as having a serious corruption problem. Moreover, Hanstad and Prosterman had heard anecdotes from other NGOs working in India that gave them pause. For instance, even something as simple as registering a power of attorney was likely to be difficult in India, and might even lead to a request for a substantial bribe.

If RDI decided to enter India, Hanstad was fairly certain that he and his family would need to live there so that he could open and oversee RDI's Indian office. While his family was open to the opportunity, he wondered if it would really be worth all of the hassle. He commented:

> As foreigners, for instance, we would need to register with the police when we first moved to India. We had heard that this was an incredibly long, arduous process that could take days and days, and in the end we would probably be asked for a bribe. Every member of my family would have to go in and register, and then we would have to go through the process all over again every time we entered or exited the country. . . . Let's just say that we had heard that working as foreigners in India would require a great deal of fortitude.

While these concerns were real, Prosterman and Hanstad also knew that they had considerable experience in overcoming such challenges. In Russia, RDI had flourished despite comparably difficult circumstances. Hanstad reflected, "We would never have pursued work in Russia if we had listened to all of the advice we were given about the local governments. . . . Everyone said the courts are corrupt, etc., etc. We decided to go ahead, and we managed to achieve great success there."

The Opportunities in Working with Governments of Developing Countries

Prosterman and Hanstad recognized that these challenges would, at the same time, provide RDI with the opportunity to achieve significant impact: RDI could potentially help to educate and transform local government officials in India. RDI's work in Moldova and Ukraine provided an instructive example. Prosterman reflected:

We had an opportunity to educate government officials in Moldova and Ukraine, and this was as important as our direct program work. Sometimes NGOs have a culture of seeing developing-country governments as the problem and the enemy; in some instances this can be a suboptimal approach by preventing the nonprofit from working with the government. . . . You can catch more flies with honey than with vinegar. . . . There are lawful and effective ways of trying to nudge governments by working with them, even those who perform badly.

Hanstad nodded in agreement, observing:

I'm always amazed at how many nonprofits choose the most difficult path. . . . My advice to nonprofits is not to let the best be the enemy of the good. Many nonprofits have an ideological view of what is best, and these purists often miss opportunities to effect positive change. . . . Currently in India, there are many occasions in which NGOs should be working with and through governments . . . and they do not to their detriment.

Of course, the extent to which it was helpful or even necessary that an NGO work with local governments depended in part on the type of program being carried out. Large microcredit programs, for instance, could be carried out without government involvement. In contrast, the nature of RDI's work necessitated working with governments; bringing RDI programs to scale required strong involvement from the host-country government.

Over the years, RDI developed effective approaches to working with developing country governments. Prosterman described the approach:

We find key champions in the local governments that have overlapping agendas with ours. . . . We will gravitate toward those things and develop relationships with those government officials . . . this has primed us for other work. When RDI first started working in China, for example, we realized that we'd make enemies by focusing on land ownership . . . so we tried to look at where the Chinese were pushing and push them a bit further, toward long-term rights that have 75 to 95 percent of the economic value of full ownership. We decided that a significant something was better than an absolute nothing. As a general rule, we are willing to sit down with any party or stakeholder and talk to him. . . . We don't go in speaking loudly and interrupting news conferences . . . we go in quietly, feeling passionately about the issues . . . we have gained the trust of government officials because they know that we won't talk to the press and make them look bad.

Prosterman and Hanstad reviewed the pros and cons once more as they prepared to make their decision. The opportunity in India was tremendous—if they were successful, they could impact an enormous number of people, offering hope of a better life to millions. On the other hand, the challenges were very real, and RDI did not have a revenue source to support an entry into India. Their decision would have a substantial impact on the future of RDI.

QUESTIONS

1. *Would you have advised RDI to enter India when the organization was considering it in 1999? Why or why not?*
2. *What can be learned from RDI's decision to pass up the urban land reform opportunity in the former Soviet Union?*
3. *How does the international context present greater challenges and opportunities for nonprofit organizations than they would face were they working solely in a developed country, such as the United States? How can these challenges and opportunities best be addressed?*

Exhibit 1
RDI Mission, Vision, and Values

RDI's mission, vision, and values, as described on the organization's Web site.

MISSION
What We Do

RDI works to secure land rights for the world's poorest people—those 3.4 billion, chiefly rural, people who live on less than two dollars a day. RDI partners with developing countries to design and implement laws, policies, and programs concerning land that provide opportunity, further economic growth, and promote social justice.

VISION
Why We Do This

We envision a world free of poverty. We see a future in which all who depend on land for their well-being have secure land rights—one of the most basic, powerful resources for lifting oneself and one's family out of poverty.

VALUES

We succeed because we believe

- Eliminating global poverty is possible and is squarely within our moral, economic, and security interests.
- All poor and marginalized people deserve respect, dignity, and meaningful opportunities to improve their well-being.

- Law is a powerful and highly leveraged tool for social and economic change.

- Land is the most critical asset for a majority of the world's poorest people.

- The lack of secure land rights is a root cause of global poverty.

- Secure land rights provide a foundation for better living conditions.

- Women deserve equal land rights.

- A small group of individuals working together, motivated by common purposes, and fueled by passion and a commitment to professionalism can take on the world's biggest problems and make a positive difference.

Source: http://www.rdiland.org (accessed February 15, 2007).

Exhibit 2
RDI Results, As of 1999

Nation	Years	Families Benefited	Household Size	# of People Benefited	Land Allocated (acres)
South Vietnam	1970–73	1,000,000	5.4	5,400,000	3,325,000
Philippines	1972–80	200,000	5.4	1,100,000	850,000
El Salvador	1980–84	50,000	6.0	300,000	175,000
Egypt	1985–92	50,000	5.0	250,000	100,000
Russia	1992–	26,000,000	3.5	91,000,000	14,175,000
Kyrgyzstan	1992–	200,000	6.0	1,200,000	3,375,000
China	1996–	42,500,000	4.42	187,000,000	40,250,000
Moldova	1997–	35,000	3.5	120,000	250,000
		70,000,000		**286,000,000**	**62,250,000**

Source: *RDI 1999 Annual Report*, p. 7.

Exhibit 3
RDI Functional Expenses, 1999
(All values in $)

	Program and Management	Fund-Raising	Total
Salaries, Wages, and Related Expenses	769,428	61,240	830,668
Other Expenses			
Foreign Partners	83,204	0	83,204
Research Consultants	33,608	0	33,608
Travel	225,219	8,441	233,660
Domestic Office	61,976	0	61,976
Foreign Offices/Housing	30,961	0	30,961
Telephone and Fax	24,684	424	25,108
Professional Services	75,139	4,068	79,207
Printing and Duplicating	4,621	2,950	7,571
Office Expense	40,973	3,240	44,213
Depreciation	16,105	0	16,105
Other Expenses	37,013	1,081	38,094
Total Expenses	**1,402,931**	**81,444**	**1,484,375**

Source: *RDI 1999 Annual Report*, p. 26.

Exhibit 4
RDI Board of Directors, 1999

In 1999, the RDI board consisted of the following members:

John E. Corbally, Chair
Chairman, The John D. & Catherine T. MacArthur Foundation
Richard B. Cray, Treasurer
Chairman, Primus Corporation
Chuck Shelton, Secretary
CEO, Diversity Management, Inc.
Janet Curry
President of the Board, Santa Fe Rape Crisis Center
Laura Lee Grace
President, Grace Interior Design
George Kargianis
Senior Partner, Kargianis Watkins Marler
Hen-Pin "Ping" Kiang
Attorney, Perkins Coie, LLP
Michael B. King
Attorney, Lane Powell Spears Luborsky
Whitney MacMillan
Director Emeritus, Cargill, Inc.
Margaret A. Niles
Attorney, Preston Gates & Ellis
James C. Pigott
Chairman and CEO, Management Reports & Services
William R. Robinson
Attorney
Robert F. Utter
Supreme Court Justice (Retired), State of Washington Supreme Court

Source: *RDI 1999 Annual Report*, p. 23.

Case Number 8

The Future of Mt. Hillyer College

The 150-year celebrations at Mt. Hillyer College had gone off without a hitch. They had come to an end a few hours earlier when, after giving the commencement speech and receiving an honorary doctorate, the president of the United States had taken off in Air Force One. Soon students, parents, and guests had departed as well. And now, in the long twilight hours of a beautiful June evening, Mt. Hillyer College was again quiet.

But there were still a few people in the President's House, sitting on the porch and relaxing from a strenuous week. They were the people who, for a whole year, had worked on the anniversary week: the president of the college, Dr. Leonides, a young, energetic man, and his wife, the head of the Psychology Department; the president emeritus, old Dr. Langton, who had built Mt. Hillyer into its present size, eminence, and prosperity after he took over the sleepy, small school right after World War II; the chairwoman of the board of trustees, Judge Catherine Holman of the state's supreme court, and the college's most distinguished living graduate, her husband, the dean of the state university's prestigious law school; the dean of the faculty; the dean of students; a few other senior administrators; and the student body president.

The president emeritus, as was his wont, went around the group asking them what each thought had been the most important happening of the week. Finally, he turned to the chairwoman's husband, the law school dean, and said, "Dean Holman, you are the only outsider here; yet you haven't said a word. What do you consider the most important or most interesting event of the last week?"

Holman smiled and said: "You know to me the most interesting thing was something that did NOT happen. Everybody talked about the past of Mt. Hillyer, its accomplishments, its many firsts, its glories. No one talked about the future. To be sure, we had a good talk on the future of liberal education—witty, erudite, inspirational. But it really only told us that liberal education is good. Mt. Hillyer is a pretty big place by now, at least for a private undergraduate school. Thanks mainly to the two of you, Dr. Langton and Dr. Leonides, it now has 4,500 students. When my wife went here, you had no more than 450 to 500. It has a name and a reputation and a good endowment for its size. But what is its excellence going to be tomorrow? Or doesn't it need such a thing? Can it be content with being like everyone else, only a little more so?

"In a law school we know—or think we do—what we are trying to do. And while the number of graduates who pass the bar examination is hardly a good measurement, at least it is a measurement. I know there are some attractive features to Mt. Hillyer—it's lovely country out there. But is that enough? The people who started and built Mt. Hillyer—we heard a lot about them these last few days—wouldn't have thought so. They had a goal when they started a school in what was then a godforsaken wilderness on the very edge of the beyond. And their successors, who in the late nineteenth century cut the college loose from church affiliation, went coeducational, and pushed science and government and economics, also had a pretty clear idea of what the college was supposed to stand for.

"I don't expect you to come up with answers. But I am a little disturbed that no one this past week has been asking any questions. Most of the work of higher education in this country is already being done in large, urban mass institutions, tax-supported. Is it enough for Mt. Hillyer to be small, private (and thereby expensive), and still semirural? Or do you have to stand for something in higher education? Should it be excellence in teaching? Should it be leadership in new areas of learning and knowledge? Should it be close integration with the world of work, the adult world which students, as a rule, know nothing of—for instance, through an organized work program for students during three months of the year? Or is it enough to try to get a few faculty members with big reputations and then to be selective in admitting students who have both the money and the grades? "But," said Dean Holman, "my real concern is how one asks these questions—or perhaps my real concern is that we in higher education don't ask them, as a rule, but make instead speeches about the glories of liberal education."

QUESTIONS

Are these legitimate concerns, do you think? And can one come to grips with them—or can one only make speeches about them?

Case Number 9

The Water Museum*

Jacob Peters was a successful businessman who, to give back to the community, served on a variety of volunteer nonprofit boards. A natural leader, he quickly became the chairman of many of the boards on which he served. When he began serving on a local water utility board, he quickly rose to a leadership position. Within a few years, he was elected to serve as chairman, a highly coveted position with a broad range of responsibilities.

The utility had recently begun construction on a massive reservoir in a remote but growing area in the region. Much to everyone's surprise, there were tremendous historical finds on the site. The utility was working with a local community-based foundation that had offered to construct a museum adjacent to the reservoir to house the historical finds. The utility provided a long-term lease in exchange for the foundation's constructing and operating the museum to showcase the historical items.

Jacob saw the value of developing an educational facility and quickly decided that the utility should also construct a museum to educate future generations on the importance of water conservation. There was wide support among the other board members for the museum. The utility board decided it would be more efficient and effective to establish a separate organization with the sole purpose of developing and operating the water museum.

* This case was prepared by Marguerite Wheeler of the Peter F. Drucker and Masatoshi Ito Graduate School of Management under the supervision of Joseph A. Maciariello, November 2007.

The board created a nonprofit organization, the museum board, and filed with the Internal Revenue Service so that donations made to the museum would be deductible as charitable contributions under IRS Code Section 170. The majority of the members of the utility board believed that a separate entity would also have greater success in fund-raising and in seeking public and private grants. The board thought grants might be more readily available to support a nonprofit water education center and museum than to support a program of a water utility.

The utility board appointed members to the museum board. These members had diverse professional backgrounds and were all successful leaders in their respective professions. The board consisted of five directors, including a private consultant, an educator, an architect, and two utility board members who served on both the museum and utility board. Jacob Peters was elected to chair the museum board at its first meeting.

The utility board granted the museum board a long-term lease of several acres of land adjacent to the site leased to the local foundation. The campus would be developed as a facility to educate visitors on water and on the historical items found at the reservoir site. The museum board quickly began fund-raising and successfully raised millions of dollars through state, federal, and local grants, including a grant from another regional utility.

At one meeting the board established its mission statement. The purposes of the museum included advancing public knowledge of water-related issues, communicating information about the history of water in the region, and emphasizing the importance of water management and conservation. After much discussion, the board agreed on the following mission statement of the museum:

To promote among the general public an awareness and appreciation of water related issues—past, present, and future—and to provide leadership in research leading to more efficient water usage.

They also identified their target audience as

a spectrum of visitors across several categories: students (grades kindergarten through 6), students (grades 7 through 12), post-secondary students, family units, senior citizens, foreign tourists, utility and/or business professionals, educators, chambers of commerce members, and government leaders.

Two years later, the museum board had developed plans for its facility and was ready to begin construction. The board went back to the utility board to provide an update and to ask for a loan, which would allow them to construct the water museum. The utility board was very supportive and voted to grant the museum board enough money to construct the facility and its exhibits. Jacob Peters immediately called a meeting of the museum board to initiate construction and to develop a business plan, including a fund-raising plan, to ensure that the museum would be ready to operate once completed.

The museum board appointed six additional board members in the hope of raising additional funds through contacts and increased involvement of business leaders. Each successful in his or her own career, the new members had ties to leaders and politicians in the community.

Construction progressed steadily on the project, but the museum board found fund-raising to be very challenging. Two years later, the facility was nearing completion, but no additional funds had been raised. Construction costs were higher than estimated owing to a building boom in the region.

Peters realized that while they could complete construction, there was not going to be enough money to open the facility. More than four years after construction began, the museum board was unable to raise any additional funds. The museum was completed, but the board did not have funds to hire staff and to operate the facility. Finally, Peters called a meeting of the museum board to discuss the future of the facility, which had not opened to the public.

QUESTIONS

Does the mission of the museum meet the three "musts" of a successful mission? Did the museum board define the market? Can it be successful in reaching a diverse audience? As the leader of a start-up that is not prepared to operate, what should Jacob Peters do? What would you do if you were on the museum board? What would you do if you were on the utility board?

Case Number 10

Should the Water Utility Operate a Museum?*

Auggie O'Farrell had served on a local water utility board for over two decades. He had dreamed of one day serving as chairman of the board and was eventually elected to the highly coveted position. He was elected during a particularly challenging time for the utility. The challenges included resource uncertainty, increasing water rates, threats of deregulation, and an aging workforce. Twenty years of service on the board gave Auggie a unique perspective, and he quickly started to implement strategies to address the many challenges.

The utility had recently begun construction of a massive reservoir in a remote but growing area in the region. Much to everyone's surprise, there were numerous historical finds on the site. The utility was working with a local community-based foundation that had offered to construct a museum adjacent to the reservoir to house the historical finds. The utility provided a long-term lease in exchange for an agreement with the foundation that it construct and operate the museum to showcase the historical items.

The person whose term had preceded Auggie's as chairman had envisioned another education center, one that would be operated by the utility, to provide education on the importance of conserving water

---

* This case was prepared by Marguerite Wheeler of the Peter F. Drucker and Masatoshi Ito Graduate School of Management under the supervision of Professor Joseph A. Maciariello, January 2008.

for future generations. There had been wide support for the project among the other board members. The utility board decided it would be more efficient and effective to establish an organization whose sole purpose was to develop and operate a water museum, completely separate from the utility. The board created a nonprofit organization, a museum board, and filed with the Internal Revenue Service so that donations made to the museum would be deductible as charitable contributions under IRS Code Section 170. The majority of the members of the utility board believed that a separate, nonprofit organization would enjoy greater success at fund-raising and in seeking public and private grants to support the establishment of a water education center and museum.

The utility board granted the museum board a long-term lease of several acres of land adjacent to the site leased to the community-based foundation. The campus would be developed as a facility to educate visitors on water issues and on the historical items found at the reservoir site. The museum board quickly began fund-raising and successfully raised millions of dollars through state, federal, and local grants, as well as a grant from another regional utility.

Four years later, the facility was nearing completion, but the museum board had not raised operating funds because their attention had been focused on completing construction. As a result, they had a brand-new facility, with no funds to hire staff or to operate the museum!

Auggie realized that although the utility had many pressing issues, this one could galvanize his board. He met with the chairman of the museum board, a man who had served on the utility board for several years, to discuss alternate options regarding the museum. The museum board then requested a loan to allow the museum to open and run the facility for five years, with the utility releasing funds for the operation of the museum as the museum reached predetermined milestones. At the end of the term, if the museum board had not repaid the loan or was not self-sufficient, the facility would revert back to the utility. Auggie then met with his executive committee to discuss options for the utility board regarding the museum. After long discussion, the committee arrived at four options:

1. Loan the funds to the museum.

2. Provide a grant to the museum.

3. Take possession of the museum.

4. Take no action.

The executive committees settled on option four; it took no action. Within a few months, the museum board had to transfer the facility to the utility because they lacked funds to operate the museum. Auggie called a meeting of his executive committee to determine how to proceed. The executive committee elected to hire a consultant with experience operating museums to develop additional options for the utility board to consider. The facility reopened using the utility staff and resources while awaiting the analysis and options of the consultant.

Several months later, the consultant reported back with the following options for the utility board to consider:

1. Maintain ownership of the facility and utilize it as a visitors' center for the adjacent reservoir. This would require ongoing operating funds but would give the utility control over the facility.

2. Partner with another nonprofit organization to operate the facility. This could provide outside funding over time and lessen the financial burden on the utility, but with the risk that the selected nonprofit would face financial difficulties in the future. The partner would have to complement the community-based foundation adjacent to the facility; otherwise the utility could end up inheriting still another nonprofit organization.

3. Convert the facility to commercial use and sell it to an interested party. The facility was unique, and the utility would risk losing control of the use of the facility and creating a negative impact on the adjacent community-based foundation.

As Auggie prepared for the board meeting, he was contacted by many of the board members and quickly realized that the board was split. Some directors had visited the museum and saw a long-term use for it by the utility, while others felt equally strongly that the utility had no business operating a museum. Millions of dollars had already been spent by the facility that could have been used more effectively to serve the mission of the utility.

Reflecting on his experience as a board member, Auggie began to realize that this issue could impact many other issues the utility faced. Alliances had formed on the board, revolving around the issue of the museum, that could continue well past the vote on the museum.

QUESTIONS

What should Auggie do? How would you vote as a director? Is there a time when an organization should engage in business that is not part of its mission?

Case Number 11

Meeting the Growing Needs of the Social Sector

According to Thomas Tierney—chairman of the Bridgespan Group, a nonprofit organization designed to provide general management consulting services to foundations and other nonprofits—approximately one hundred nonprofit organizations are created every day in the United States and foundations are being formed at the rate of approximately three thousand each year. Volunteerism in America recently hit a thirty-year high, with 27 percent of Americans claiming that they volunteer on a regular basis. Charitable giving has hit approximately $300 billion, up from $120 billion a few years ago.*

Peter Drucker, perhaps more than any other single person, worked to professionalize the management of social-sector organizations. Over his long and productive life, Peter Drucker consulted with leaders of large and small social-sector organizations, such as the American Red Cross, the Salvation Army, the Girl Scouts, Catholic Charities, CARE, and numerous hospitals and churches. Yet near the end of his life, he expressed the view that because social-sector organizations do not have an adequate definition of results (such as profit), they are more vulnerable to mismanagement

---

* Thomas Tierney is chairman of the Bridgespan Group and former CEO of Bain & Co. This information was contained in the keynote address by Mr. Tierney at a conference sponsored by the Drucker Institute and the Leader to Leader Institute, on November 19, 2007, in New York City.

than are business organizations. In fact, he thought them still to be by-and-large poorly managed.*

Peter Drucker expressed his hopes for social-sector institutions upon the formation of the Peter F. Drucker Foundation for Nonprofit Management (now the Leader to Leader Institute).** These aspirations are described in the remainder of this case.

"Our Foundation hopes to concentrate on our priorities as they are emerging from both what we think we are—or should be—good at and from what we get as the main need and result areas from the (somewhat overwhelming) response to the announcement of the Foundation's birth.

"One priority area—maybe the top one, judging from the responses we have been getting—is the development of ways in which a nonprofit organization (and especially one of the smaller ones) can evaluate itself: its mission, its performance and results, its structure and organization, the allocation of its resources, and—badly needed— its performance in attracting and using resources, both people and money. This will have to be a self-evaluation tool kit. But—and all of us agreed—it will surely lead toward some follow-up, whether a reference service to help nonprofits get the kind of outside help (e.g., a consultant) they might need to work on areas that need change or strengthening, or a list of resources such as businesspeople available to help, or perhaps, in the end, a consulting service of our own, perhaps even a profitmaking subsidiary. The demand for this is so great that we, reluctantly, have come to the conclusion that this, however difficult, has to be a major priority.

"Another area of concentration should be the development of information—information on available materials, whether books, pe-

---

* See "Peter F. Drucker on Mission-Driven Leadership and Management in the Social Sector, Interviews and Postscripts, by Joseph A. Maciariello," *The Journal of Management, Spirituality & Religion, Special Issue, Values and Virtues in Organizations*, Vol. 3, Issues 1 and 2, 2006.

** These hopes were enumerated as a part of a letter from Peter Drucker to Mr. David A. Jones, Chairman & CEO, Humana Inc., Louisville, Kentucky, October 26, 1990. Source: The Drucker Institute.

riodicals, people, videos, and so on, for nonprofit organizations. There is tremendous demand for this, and the work would have to be done, I imagine, in partnership with major information and database suppliers. This sounds mundane—and it is. But, we have found out that the need is very great.

"A third area is what we have come to call "parallel careers." A number of organizations, for example, the National Executive Service Corps, place retired business executives into nonprofit assignments, usually full-time, for a short period of time such as a year. But there is a much larger group of people—usually younger ones—who want to find the right kind of non-profit volunteer work while staying in their work and job. Within the church segment of the third (or social) sector, these people usually—or often—place themselves; they have been members of the congregation for years and now become highly active volunteers. Otherwise, however, there is no other organization that even attempts to match the strengths, values, and experiences of the person with the needs of a nonprofit institution. The tools for doing this exist: the National Executive Service Corps has developed—and highly successfully—fairly simple methods for finding out both the individual's strengths and the institution's values and needs, and then matching the two—and they will make these tools available to us (they want to work closely with the Foundation as we clearly complement what they have been doing since 1976). And there are good analytical tools available for the individual: Dick Bolles's *What Color Is Your Parachute** or what Bernie Haldana developed thirty years ago in his placement work. But, so far, they have not been adapted and applied to the parallel career or to placement with a nonprofit organization altogether. Mismatches are more common than the right fit and there is a contribution to be made.

"There is a fourth area—so far, I fear, still quite nebulous (and probably still in the future)—the central clearinghouse for nonprofit management. Any number of nonprofit organizations have come to

---

* Now in its eighth edition (2004) with total sales in excess of 8 million copies.

us at the Foundation and said, we desperately need to find out what is available, what other organizations are doing, what works—in fund-raising, in creating an effective board, in managing volunteers, in defining the mission, in defining results. I think that this function may, in the end, be one of the most important things we can do—it was the most important thing the American Management Association did in the 1950s. But, it needs both meetings in which people get together under expert leadership and a very substantial information base—and both need time.

"I have not been explicit about what the Foundation is likely to do BEST. I think that is the crucial question—but it may be too early for us to answer it. I have tried to outline what I think our priorities might be, judging by both the need of the customers and their receptivity. It is up to us to learn how to excel in serving the customers, we do know, however, that the MARKET is there, provided we can achieve excellence—and that is what we are fully committed to. And let me say that the people leading the effort are fully committed to doing things right."

ASSIGNMENT

Peter Drucker applied the principles of "Drucker on Management" to the needs of the social sector by establishing the practices of the foundation that bore his name (until it morphed into the Leader to Leader Institute).

Consult the Web sites of other organizations carrying out work in the social sector, including, but not limited to, the ones mentioned in this case, and make your own assessment of the needs and status of the organizations comprising this sector. What role might you play now and in the future in this sector?

Case Number 12

The Dilemma of Aliesha State College: Competence versus Need

Until the 1970s, Aliesha was a well-reputed, somewhat sleepy state teachers college located on the outer fringes of a major metropolitan area. Then, with the rapid expansion of college enrollments, the state converted Aliesha to a four-year state college (and the plans called for its becoming a state university with graduate work and perhaps even with a medical school in the early 1990s). Within ten years, Aliesha grew from 1,500 to 9,000 students. Its budget expanded even faster than the enrollment, increasing twentyfold during that period.

The only part of Aliesha that did not grow was the original part, the teachers college; there enrollment actually went down. Everything else seemed to flourish. In addition to building new four-year schools of liberal arts, business, veterinary medicine, dentistry, Aliesha developed many community service programs. Among them were a rapidly growing evening program, a mental-health clinic, and a speech therapy center for children with speech defects—the only one in the area. Even within education one area grew—the demonstration high school attached to the old teachers college. Even though it enrolled only 300 students, this high school was taught by the leading experts in teacher education and was considered the best high school in the whole area.

Then in 1996 the budget was suddenly cut quite sharply by the state legislature. At the same time the faculty demanded and got a fairly hefty raise in salary. It was clear that something had to give—the budget deficit was much too great to be covered by ordinary cost reductions. When the faculty committee sat down with the president and the board of trustees, two candidates for abandonment emerged after long and heated wrangling: the speech-therapy program and the demonstration high school. Both cost about the same—and both were extremely expensive.

The speech-therapy clinic, everyone agreed, addressed itself to a real need and one of high priority. But—and everybody had to agree, as the evidence was overwhelming—it did not do the job. Indeed, it did such a poor, sloppy, disorganized job that pediatricians, psychiatrists, and psychologists hesitated to refer their patients to the clinic. The reason was that the clinic was a college program run to teach psychology students rather than to help children with serious speech impediments.

The opposite criticism applied to the high school. No one questioned its excellence and the impact it made on the education students who listened in on its classes and on the many young teachers in the area who came in as auditors. But what need did it fill? There were plenty of perfectly adequate high schools in the area.

"How can we justify," asked one of the psychologists connected with the speech clinic, "running an unnecessary high school in which each child costs as much as a graduate student at Harvard?"

"But how can we justify," asked the dean of the School of Education, himself one of the outstanding teachers in the demonstration high school, "a speech clinic that has no results even though each of its patients costs the state as much as one of our demonstration high school students, or more?"

At this point the chairman of the board of trustees took the floor: "What I hear is that the defenders of the speech clinic argue need, though they admit incompetence and inability to correct it; for state law and our charter demand that a college activity be focused on the needs of the students, which, you tell us, makes it impossible to run a therapeutically effective speech clinic. Still, you argue need. And you," he said, turning to the defenders of the demonstration high school, "argue competence. You do make a contribution to the remaining education students but, above all, by setting standards of teaching and education that raise the level of all the high schools in our area. But the need you satisfy is minor compared to the unique need the speech clinic should be satisfying but isn't. We are not allowed by state law to cut activities below the budget given to us. Otherwise I'd move that we close down *both* the speech clinic and the demonstration high school. But we have to close one. Which deserves priority: need or competence?"

QUESTION

Which does deserve priority?

Case Number 13

What Are "Results" in the Hospital?

Robert Armstrong joined the struggling family company when he came out of the navy. A few years later, his father died suddenly and Armstrong took over what was then a very small, indeed, practically a marginal business. For more than twenty years the business took all his time—or almost all of it. For Armstrong had always had a strong interest in health care. As a youngster he had thought seriously of going to medical school and might have done so had he not been drafted while in college. He therefore began to work for one of the major community hospitals in his metropolitan area almost immediately. He was elected to the hospital's board in 1985 and became chairman of the board in 1995. Armstrong took these duties seriously and gave unstintingly of his time and energy.

By the early 2000s, the Armstrong Company had become a substantial business. Robert Armstrong, who alone had been "the management" twenty years earlier, had built what he considered an unusually competent management team. Though Armstrong was still in his early fifties, business had begun to bore him. He had also begun to resent the heavy travel schedule that the business imposed on him.

When the administrator of the hospital suddenly suffered a stroke and had to retire, the Board appointed a selection committee to choose a replacement and named Robert Armstrong its chairman.

Before the first meeting of the committee, Armstrong met with the hospital's chief of Medical Services—a respected physician who had also for many years been Armstrong's personal doctor—to decide with him what kind of a man the committee should be looking for. To Armstrong's total surprise, the doctor said, "Look, Bob, cut out the nonsense. You don't have to look for the man to head up St. Luke's. You are the man. No one knows more about the place than you do. No one is better accepted. And I know—you told me so last October at your annual physical—that your present job bores you, that they don't need you in the company anymore, and that you and Libby are tired of your eternal traveling. All right, so you are making a great deal more dough as president of Armstrong than we pay a hospital administrator. But you have enough money and don't need a big income. Hospital administrators aren't that badly paid. They make as much as you pay your vice presidents—at least that's what you told us when we last raised the administrator's salary in the board meeting six months ago."

The more Armstrong thought about this, the more sense it made to him. But also, the more he thought, the more uneasy he became about his ability to do the job. He went back to the doctor and said, "If I take this job, how do I measure my performance? What results should I be after? What is performance in a hospital, and what are results?"

The doctor grinned broadly and said, "I knew you'd ask those questions and that's why I'd love to see you take the job. I know what results are in my work and in my practice. But neither I nor anyone else knows what they are for the hospital. Maybe it's time some disagreeable type like you asks these questions."

Armstrong took the job and soon became known as one of the most effective and accomplished hospital managers in the country. Six years later, the American College of Hospital Administrators named him Hospital Administrator of the Year. In his short acceptance speech Armstrong said: "To take the job as hospital administrator was the most intelligent thing I did in my whole life—it's been a wonderful six years. But the one question I came in to answer, I still can't answer. In fact, I am more confused now than I was six years ago. I know now that a modern big-city hospital has a multitude of objectives and serves a multitude of customers and clients: the doctors, who look upon the hospital as an extension of their practice; the patients, who expect us to cure them or at least not to harm them; their families; the community; the various agencies—governments, Blue Cross, insurance companies, employers, unions, and so on—who pay our bills; and many others. I know that we are expected to remedy damage that has already been done, the one job we are reasonably good at. But we are increasingly expected to be the community's health care center and to help keep healthy people healthy. Increasingly we are expected to substitute for the private physician in treating the poor, especially in the inner city.

"I have given up the hope of finding one performance goal and one performance measurement. But what bothers me is that I really don't know how to measure performance in any one of these missions. I do not know how to define what is 'good performance' in any area, what to strive for, what to give priority to, and what to abandon or play down. With 14 percent of the country's national product going to health care—and the cost going up—health care is too important not to have objectives, performance standards, and measurements. But can any one of you experienced hospital administrators in the audience tell me what objectives, goals, standards, and measurements you are using or which ones I might try using?"

QUESTIONS

Is there any way to tackle Armstrong's question? Or is "health care" so intangible as to defy definitions, objectives, and measurement?

Case Number 14

Cost Control in the Hospital

It took only ten days for Seymour Politz to get the following reply to the letter he had sent to his cousin Linda:

Dear Seymour:

I am delighted to give you my opinion of the expansion plans for Glen River Hospital, of which you are Chairman of the Finance Committee (which I didn't know). I am impressed by your excellent planning. Indeed, I intend to use your projections of population trends in relation to hospital needs as the model for my staff here. We are just about to develop guidelines for hospital planning for our state. So Glen River's plans are coming in very handy indeed. And please give Dr. Bernauer, your Administrator, my best regards and my compliments on an excellent job of planning. I knew the plans would be a model the moment I saw his name on them; I remember vividly the contribution he made when he and I sat together on the President's Committee on Military Hospitals.

I do indeed agree with Dr. Bernauer's conclusion that Glen River Hospital urgently needs to add some 30 rooms—or 60 beds—and that what you need are additional clinical-care beds. As a matter of fact, I think that your figures are low; with your population forecasts for the Glen River area, you might better aim at a minimum of 75 new clinical beds, or around 38 or 40 to semiprivate rooms. But, Seymour, you have these rooms. Or rather, you are today using some 40 clinical—and that means high-cost—rooms for purposes that require only much cheaper facilities—cheaper by two-thirds or so in respect to capital investment, cheaper by about one-half in respect to service, and cheaper also in respect to maintenance.

You have in your main hospital building clinical care rooms reserved for maternity. Childbirth is not a disease; all the healthy mother needs is a place to lie down and sleep off the fatigue. And she should move around, have something to do. In other words, what she needs is the simplest kind of motel room, preferably with a daybed she can open or close as she wants. Some babies do need a clinical-care facility, but that's a small room and a simple one. Mothers need a place to make coffee, to sit down and to chat. And the cost of the kind of rooms you need for mothers—including an intensive-care facility for infants in trouble, delivery rooms and recovery rooms—is around one third the cost of the intensive-care rooms. Build a motel for maternity, and free the maternity rooms you now use for clinical-care patients. Similarly, you have 10 rooms for mental patients—and you don't admit any serious cases. You admit people with depressions, people with anxieties, people who need counseling or protection against a demanding world. They should be forced to move around, eat in a cafeteria, see other people—again a small motel with some extra rooms for counseling and group therapy is what you need, rather than clinical rooms. Finally, you are using 15 rooms—perhaps more—for surgical patients, especially in orthopedic surgery and orthopedic treatment such as traction for people with serious back pain. This does not require clinical care. The person who has had ankle surgery is kept in the hospital only because the cast shouldn't dry too fast—so he stays three days until he can put weight on the cast. The woman with a bad back needs traction six or ten hours a day for two or three days—but she doesn't need clinical care; she needs a bed to lie on with the leg in the air. You do need operating rooms for these patients (you plan on 5 additional ones anyhow), you do need a recovery room, and you do need a hospital-type bed to make it easier for the nurse. But you do not need the expensive clinical care hospital room. You need something quite simple and much cheaper.

So I advise that you redraw your plans and build a 35–40-room two-story motel—70–80 beds on a semiprivate basis—at the lowest possible cost. I estimate it at around 40 percent of what you have budgeted for your expansion. And that should include the cost of refurbishing the 42-bed clinical rooms you now misuse for maternity, mental patients, and surgical recovery into the clinical-care rooms you need—that would give you all you need and a little more at much less cost; yet you'd have better facilities.

One more thing, Seymour; your plan proposes to raise all the money Glen River Hospital needs through a fund-raising campaign and as charitable contributions. That's folly and vanity. It costs much too much. In such a campaign, thirty cents or so of every dollar raised is spent on campaign costs. And then half the people who promise to give are never heard from. The only sensible way—and the only cheap one—is to borrow commercially as much as you can. You should be able to get 90 percent of your needs from banks, insurance companies, the dormitory authority of your state, Uncle Sam, and so on—and at reasonable interest rates. After all, 90 percent of your cost is underwritten by insurance companies, Blue Cross, and the government. The last 10 percent—that's what one uses philanthropy for. To use it for anything else cannot be justified in today's hospital.

Give my love to Kathy-Ann; tell her we already look forward to your visit this fall. And Jim wants me to tell you that he expects you to have a few days to go fishing with him. He has invented a new fly he is most eager to show off to you. Until then

> *As always yours,*
> *Linda Politz Buxbaum, MD*
> *Associate Commissioner of*
> *　　Hospitals*
> *State of . . .*

Seymour Politz was delighted—the letter confirmed the hunch that had led him to write to Linda in the first place. When he had received Dr. Bernauer's proposal for expanding Glen River Hospital two weeks ago, he had been quite upset. The proposal called for three times as much money as he had anticipated. He himself had intended to contribute heavily. But although he was a fairly wealthy man, the projected costs were many times what he could contribute. To raise that large a sum through a fund drive seemed to him almost impossible, especially with the concern in the town of Glen River over rising hospital costs. But 40 percent of the amount Bernauer proposed—and most of it borrowed from the banks—that would be no problem. He himself could surely make up the difference between what the banks would lend and what would be needed.

And so he went to see Dr. Bernauer at the hospital. "Yes," said Bernauer, "I know all this—though your cousin, as usual, is a little quicker than most of us are. But, Seymour, it won't work even though it makes sense. The other trustees are never going to agree to borrowing from the banks and insurance companies at commercial rates. They'll tell you that once you do this, you can't raise money any more through a charity drive—people will say, 'if they can get money from the banks, why should I give?' I think the trustees are wrong—people are a little brighter than that. But you'll see that the trustees will flatly refuse to do anything but pass the hat, no matter how expensive it is. But your greatest obstacle," continued the administrator, "will be the physicians. Maybe some of the surgeons will go along. There are now a few freestanding surgical clinics run on the same principle, although all of them are profit-making ventures and I haven't heard of surgeons in nonprofit community hospitals like ours accepting the idea of a semi-ambulatory and cheap surgical facility. But the obstetricians and the psychiatrists and the psychologists are going to yell bloody murder. You are downgrading them and their skill; if their patients aren't truly 'very sick' people, then they won't be respected as true healers."

Politz didn't believe the administrator. But after a few talks—with fellow trustees, with the chief of obstetrics and the chief of psychiatry—he learned that the administrator was right. So, downcast, he went back to Dr. Bernauer and asked, "Is there anything we can do?"

"Oh sure," said Bernauer, "sell the hospital to a profit-making hospital corporation or convert it into a profit-making hospital owned by our doctors; and, presto, there won't be any trouble." "You are a cynic," said Politz. "No, I don't think so," said Bernauer. "Sure, some doctors are too greedy. But the profits they'd make as owners of Glen River Hospital are so trivial as to make no difference to any of them. And it isn't *their* profits that would make them change their minds anyhow. What your cousin Linda recommends is being done at the other end of the metropolitan area at St. Vincent's, which the nuns sold to a hospital company in St. Louis last year.

"There the doctors accept and support it, even though they have no share in the ownership and in and profits. I have been thinking about this for a long time," said Bernauer. "It bothers me. I think I can explain it. In a community nonprofit hospital like ours, low costs and efficiency aren't values. The trustees glory in the good cause and are really upset if you point out that we are very much like a business or should be. Why should they then sit on the board and give of their time and money? And the physicians are much too far away from financial results. If they own the hospital, they see revenues as meaningful. If a company owns it, they respect—maybe over-respect—the businessman. But if it's a community hospital and a good cause, well, you don't put a price tag on good works. . . . "

QUESTIONS

What do you think of Dr. Bernauer's explanation? And by the way, could Politz and Bernauer do anything to change the attitude and point of view of the trustees and the physicians? And if they have no success—and few attempts of this kind have been successful—should they go ahead with building the very expensive clinical-care beds and with raising the money through an extremely expensive, if not wasteful, fund-raising campaign? Or should they instead try to have their state develop regulatory rules?

Part IV

Productive Work and Achieving Worker

Case Number 15

Work Simplification and the Marketing Executive*

Mr. P. W. Brown
Department 731
    I understand that the report below was written by one of your engineers after a recent symphony concert. I want to compliment you on inspiring such zeal for constructive improvement and elimination of unnecessary waste.

> T. V. Houser**
> Chairman of the Board
> Sears, Roebuck and Company

June 16, 1955
"How To Be Efficient with Fewer Violins"
    For considerable periods the four oboe players had nothing to do. The number should be reduced and the work spread more

---

* Information for this case was provided by the Reverend John Aldridge, son of the author of this case. It is used by permission of Reverend Aldridge.
** T. V. Houser served for over thirty years with Sears, Roebuck and Co. and was an expert in marketing; see his article in the *Journal of Marketing*, Vol. 23, No. 4, p. 363. http://www.jstor.org/action/doBasicSearch?Query=T.V.+Houser&dc=All+Disciplines (accessed May 31, 2008).

evenly over the whole of the concert, thus eliminating peaks of activity.

All of the twelve violins were playing identical notes; this seems unnecessary duplication. The staff of this section should be drastically cut. If a larger volume of sound is required, it could be obtained by electronic apparatus.

Much effort was absorbed in the playing of demisemiquavers; this seems to be an unnecessary refinement. It is recommended that all notes should be rounded up to the nearest semiquaver. If this were done, it would be possible to use trainees and lower-grade operatives more extensively.

There seems to be too much repetition of some musical passages. Scores should be drastically pruned. No useful purpose is served by repeating on the horns a passage which has already been handled by the strings. It is estimated that if all redundant passages were eliminated, the whole concert time of two hours could be reduced to twenty minutes and there would be no need for an intermission.

The conductor agrees with these recommendations, but expressed the opinion that there might be some falling off in box-office receipts. In that unlikely event, it should be possible to close sections of the auditorium entirely with a consequential saving of overhead expenses, lighting, attendance, etc.

*John A. Aldridge
Director of Research
Sears, Roebuck and Co.
1946–1957*

QUESTION

In view of Mr. Houser's expertise in marketing, what do you make of his commendation of this curious piece by Aldridge?

Case Number 16

The Army Service Forces[*]

The Army Service Forces was established in early 1942 by President Franklin D. Roosevelt as one of three autonomous units of the Department of the Army. Its function was to provide services and supplies to the U.S. Army during World War II. It was reorganized after the war in June 1946 and is now called the Department of the Army Staff Support.[**]

By all accounts this autonomous unit performed admirably and made major contributions to the success of the war effort. The following is an account of the contributions of one man, Lieutenant Colonel John A. Aldridge, delivered by Brigadier General Harold A. Barnes on the occasion of Lieutenant Colonel Aldridge's receipt of the Gilbreth Medal.[†] Brigadier General Barnes served as deputy quartermaster general in the Army Service Forces.

"When I was called to speak briefly to you this evening about my friend John Aldridge, I decided to touch upon a phase of his work that does not reflect itself in the cold statistical appraisals of the work-

---

[*] Information for this case was provided by the Reverend John Aldridge, son of Colonel John Aldridge. It is used by permission of Reverend Aldridge.

[**] Pbase.com, Army Services photo. http://www.pbase.com/sfce7/image/43809017 (accessed January 15, 2008).

[†] The medal was presented on January 18, 1945, by the Society for the Advancement of Management, Washington Chapter, Washington, DC. The Gilbreth Medal is given as a tribute to the pioneering work of Frank and Lillian Gilbreth in advancing efficiency and effectiveness in business operations.

simplification and work-measurement programs in which he played so large a part. True, the figures themselves are impressive—the cumulative results of the work-simplification and work-measurement programs to the end of 1944, for example, show that some 375,000 employees were surveyed and there were about 66,000 jobs eliminated. Figures such as these do not tell the whole story without recalling the background against which these programs were projected.

"Every activity of the Army Service Forces has undergone a fantastic expansion within the last few years in order to perform one dominating function—supply. However, it is always difficult to understand the other fellow's problem except in terms our own experiences. So let me ask what your reaction would be if you were the chief executive of a large organization and were suddenly informed by your board of directors that the organization would be expanded a *hundredfold* within the next twelve months. Further, that you were to be responsible for handling this expansion, at the same time discharging all of your other duties in a satisfactory manner. I imagine that you would be very impatient with anything and everything that did not have a direct and immediate bearing on the problem of 'getting out the work.' Probably you would feel a bit skeptical about management-improvement programs—such as work simplification and work measurement. Add to this the situation the violent and unpredictable demands of a global war, with its sudden shocks and strains, and you can appreciate what a problem lay before our commanding officers. Then, for good measure, throw in critical personnel and materiel shortages. This was the job that had to be done.

"Such a situation, while it created a need for an extensive work-simplification program, also created the very factors that promoted administrative resistance to such a program. It called for dissemination of knowledge and understanding of the benefit of work simplification. It required an education in the advantages of management analysis and improvement on a scale without precedent, throughout all levels of the organization. In short, it called for a type of 'salesmanship,' let us say, of the highest order."

By successfully handling this most difficult phase of an extremely difficult job, Lieutenant Colonel Aldridge left a deep impression on the management thinking of the Army Service Forces. Executives who have received benefits through improvement of their basic operations are among the most enthusiastic supporters of the work-simplification idea, and when such executives were able to improve their performance further through work-measurement studies, it followed that they would always be better, more alert and effective executives at whatever job they were assigned.

"Let me illustrate my point by citing our own experience with the work-simplification program in the Quartermaster Corps, which was introduced in all technical services of the Army Service Forces in the early part of 1943. Now, frankly, we believed at the time that we did have good office, factory, and warehousing operations. Quartermaster operations closely parallel commercial and industrial activities. Therefore we had drawn into the corps many topflight business executives from the various fields with which we were concerned—either as commissioned officers or as civilians. In addition, many of our regular army officers were acknowledged experts in their specialized fields. We had already begun an intensive work-simplification program of our own in the office of the quartermaster general. Nevertheless, we were impressed with this work-simplification program that Lieutenant Colonel Aldridge unfolded before us.

"These two programs, each carried forward throughout the Army Service Forces, were under the technical direction of Lieutenant Colonel Aldridge, and are among the most significant contributions to improved administration and executive control that I have encountered in my army experience. They were performed on an unparalleled scale within the past two years, and the results achieved have meaning, not only for army administrators, but for all progressive business and government executives as well.

"We saw the evidence before our own eyes and in our own work that the sound, simple, and direct methods he used were easy to learn and easy to apply. I want to repeat that—*easy to learn and easy to apply.*

In my opinion, this phrase embodies John Aldridge's important contribution. His rare talent for taking complicated processes and boiling them down to their essentials—to the qualities that are the basis for their successful application—has been of immeasurable value to the Army Service Forces, and added up to a substantial contribution to the war effort.

"The results he achieved in the Quartermaster Corps were beyond our expectations. Not only did we achieve substantial savings in manhours, materials, and equipment, but we were able to make thousands of our key operating personnel aware of the benefits of management-improvement programs.

"Nor were these results peculiar to the Quartermaster Corps alone—similar results were experienced in every technical service in which this program was vigorously prosecuted. In the Quartermaster Corps, we believe the benefits of the work-simplification program to be:

1. Conservation and control of manpower through the elimination of all unnecessary work and the simplification of all necessary work.

2. Conservation of space and equipment through more effective layout and the correct and full utilization of all equipment and machinery.

3. Improvement in the approach to their work on the part of both supervisors and employees at the working level by becoming acquainted with techniques for work analysis, and the widening of management consciousness on the part of all employees throughout the organization.

"As I have said, through programs such as the materials-handling work-simplification program and the work-measurement program, it has been possible to draw the operating executives themselves into full participation in the execution of intensive management-improvement programs. In programs such as these, Lieutenant Colonel Aldridge has gone one step beyond technology. In our tremendous struggle today, the rewards go to the side with the greatest teamwork, the greatest unity. By making provision for the administrators to take part in that which had hitherto been regarded as the exclusive work of the procedures specialist and the industrial engineer, Lieutenant Colonel Aldridge probed the frontiers of true management accomplishment which lie open before us—*that of human relations.* He has recognized that procedures may be calibrated or slide-ruled, but not the people who work them, that workloads and production standards can be neatly calculated, but not human nature. Human engineering has been a subject close to my own heart for years; it was with the keenest interest that I have watched Lieutenant Colonel Aldridge develop his programs for mass improvement of the operations of our huge army administrative machine.

"If you will study his methods and programs, you will see—as I have seen—John Aldridge emphasizes the fact that every management problem is ultimately a personnel problem. He has placed great stress on the factors of understanding and enlightenment of the personnel whose work is studied, giving them his full confidence and obtaining their assistance in the execution of the job. How well he has done this is evidenced by the great honor bestowed upon him—the receipt of the Gilbreth Medal for his outstanding work in the advancement of both the science and art of management.

"We in the Army Service Forces are proud of John Aldridge. We are proud of his accomplishments as a colonel in our great army and as a technician in his chosen field in our tremendous supply operations. But we are equally proud of John Aldridge as a friendly, sympathetic, and sincere individual with whom it is a privilege to be associated.

"I thank you."

QUESTIONS

The work of scientific management as developed by Frederick Taylor ultimately led to the field of industrial engineering. John A. Aldridge (1905–1978) was an industrial engineer following Taylor's methods. Scientific management and Taylor have been widely criticized as being "dehumanizing" by structuring work so that it is "monotonous." Evaluate these claims in light of the way Aldridge carried out these methods in the Army Service Forces. How can these criticisms be reconciled with the example provided in this talk? How about in light of Case 15?

Case Number 17

How Does One Analyze and Organize Knowledge Work?

If she had had a jump rope, Susan Binkley would have skipped down the whole length of New York's Park Avenue, and in broad daylight. As it was, she pirouetted at every red light. And she did something she hadn't done since she was in junior high school: she sang out loud, anything she could remember—snatches from musicals, folk songs, nursery rhymes. Some passers-by stared; others smiled as they saw a pretty young woman so obviously happy, perhaps even in love.

But it wasn't love that made Susan dance down Park Avenue; it was success. And she was not a junior-high-school kid but twenty-nine years old, terribly serious, and a liberated career woman. Only an hour earlier, the senior vice president and second in command in the Corporate Banking Division of Citizens National Bank had called her into his office and said, "I'd like to be the first to congratulate you. The Executive Committee promoted you this morning to banking officer in the Corporate Division—less than three years after you joined as a trainee and faster than anyone has made it in all my fourteen years with the bank. And I have more good news. I know that you want your own command. And I remember that you liked the three months you spent in our Houston office. Well, Bill Harris, who heads Houston, called up a few days ago and specifically asked when you'd be available to come down as his assistant manager. And so we want you to go down as soon as you can. Bill is going on vacation in seven weeks and wants you to come early enough so that he can show you the ropes—you'll be acting manager while he is gone. And by the end of the year, we plan to bring Bill back to New York to take over a new petroleum-and-chemical-industry division. If you work out— and, Susan, I know you will, and so does Harris—you'll take over as his replacement. That's an assistant VP job and a full VP title within a year."

Well, thought Susan, I can be in Houston in two days. In fact, this saves a lot of arguments with Tommy and gives me a good reason to end this relationship without tears or scenes. But isn't it wonderful— Susan Binkley, Corporate Banking Officer; Susan Binkley, Assistant VP; Susan Binkley, Vice President—well she'd make it and be the first chair*woman* of the board of a major clearinghouse bank!

Nothing had been further from Susan's mind when she graduated from college at age twenty-two than a career in banking. She had studied art and had intended to become a commercial artist. She had not been unsuccessful, had indeed been able to support herself— well, almost—for a few years. But she had gotten awfully tired of knocking at the doors of advertising agencies for work, had gotten even more tired of drawing women's undergarments for department-store ads, and had gotten most tired of a diet of peanut-butter sandwiches, which were usually all she could afford. It was sheer accident that she heard of the Citizens National Bank looking for trainees— and for women trainees, to avoid being sued for discrimination against women. The human resource officer who interviewed her was rather skeptical of her commercial-art background but brightened when Susan mentioned a couple of computer courses she had taken in college and liked—and the bank had given orders to hire *women!* And so Susan, at age twenty-six, started as a management trainee and started at the same time to go to business school in the evenings to get her MBA; the human resource person had insisted on it as a condition of employment. To her immense astonishment, Susan found that she liked bank work—or at least most of it, for the three weeks in Letters of Credit were not much fun. And she, who had always disliked school, found that she loved the business courses, especially accounting and management. Indeed, she managed to get an A even in Statistics, and so she had graduated—only three weeks earlier—at the head of her class and had actually given the valedictorian's speech at the school's commencement. And now she was going to run the Houston office.

Bill Harris was okay, but she didn't think of him as a ball of fire. He *was* a well-trained banker, and she had learned more credit analysis from him than from anybody else in the bank. But he still thought clients should come, hat in hand, and beg for loans. What the Houston office needed was aggressive marketing. She had said that to the senior VP when she came back, had thought then that it was a mistake, but realized now that he must have agreed with her—or else he wouldn't send her to Houston. That story about Bill Harris asking for her—Bill, after three months, had still not accepted that a woman could be a banker, though he was quiet about it after a few pointed remarks on her part.

Houston could easily double its business. The customers were there, and the bank had the right services at the right price. But the office needed to be organized; Bill Harris was just managing from day to day. Fortunately, she had picked that topic for her big term paper in the management class (the prof had given her an A plus). The title was "POIM in the Banking Office," and POIM stood, of course, for Planning, Organizing, Integrating, and Measuring. So she had a starting point—and by the time Harris had gone on his vacation, she would have learned enough about the Houston office to convert this paper into an action plan. But the management prof had said something else as well: "After you have done the planning and organizing of the unit or business, you had better analyze and organize the work of individuals—and especially the work of knowledge workers. Work is done by people, not by units or companies. And knowledge work requires systematic analysis and organization even more than manual work, where we usually know what the end product should be. Knowledge work," the prof had said, "is the most important area for the application of scientific management."

"Well," said Susan, "I should begin with my own work as manager of the unit. What are the pieces? How can I improve each? What information and what tools do I need? How do the pieces fit together? After I've analyzed my own job, I'll take the two most important jobs we have—marketing loans and analyzing loan applications—and do the same with them. But it isn't a time-and-motion study I need. I need a critical analysis of all major steps in the work."

QUESTIONS

Do you think Susan is right in her approach to knowledge work? And how might one go about finding the key pieces in such work?

Case Number 18

Can One Learn to Manage Subordinates?

Tom McAvoy was twenty-seven and three years out of law school when he entered the legal department of Electro-Magnetic Induction Technology Industries as a legal researcher on an antitrust case. The company then had about $50 million in sales and operated almost exclusively in North America—and really only in the USA, as the Canadian affiliate was barely more than a sales office. By the time McAvoy was forty-five, he was associate general counsel of a company—now renamed Emitco—with sales of $1.75 billion and major operations in all developed countries, and especially in the European Common Market, where one-third of the company's sales now originated. McAvoy's father had been a diplomat, and Tom had spent much of his childhood and youth abroad before coming home to the U.S. for college and law school. He was therefore multilingual, with excellent French, German, and Spanish and adequate Italian. Negotiations and legal work in Europe thus had naturally gravitated to him. He had become the company's mainstay in the development of the European network of Emitco subsidiaries and affiliates, was a member of the management committee of Emitco-Europe, and spent about half of his time in Europe and on European business.

It was no secret to anyone in Emitco that McAvoy wanted to live in Europe. When he suggested establishing the company's European headquarters in Paris, more than one wit in the company commented that McAvoy's love for that city was the real reason for the choice. Therefore, when the company's vice president–European informed headquarters that he intended to retire on his sixtieth birthday, nine months hence, McAvoy's choice as his successor surprised no one. It also pleased the heads of the European companies who had worked closely with McAvoy over the years and had found him intelligent, well-informed, and distinctly simpatico; whereas they often had difficulties working with some of the others in Emitco headquarters— most of them small-town midwesterners who had never lived outside their own country.

McAvoy was elated, but he also worried. He was conscious of the fact that he had never before managed people—he had always been a staff specialist. And now he was going to have reporting to him nine line managers and a total of 19,000 people in nine different European countries. He therefore requested a three-month leave, ostensibly to get his teenage children into boarding schools and to move his home to Paris, but in reality to prepare himself for line-operating responsibilities. Being a conscientious man, he got a list—a very long list—of books on personnel management and read them all. But the more he read, the more confused he became. The books were full of procedures, but McAvoy was fully determined to leave procedures to the personnel department. Otherwise they all talked of the kind of man he should be or should become. But what was he supposed to *do*? He knew that he had to establish himself, fairly fast: he had seen enough people get a promotion to know that one had to establish oneself in a new job within a few months or so. He knew that the only aspect of the job that was new to him was managing people—but it was *totally* new to him.

And he felt strongly that he had to know in advance what *to* do and what *not to* do: he knew that improvisation wasn't his way of doing things.

Finally, with most of the three months of his leave used up, he reluctantly went for advice and counsel to the retired chairman of the Emitco board, the man who had originally hired him. At the time

Jonathan Forbes had been an executive vice president. He had then soon become president and chief executive officer and the main architect of Emitco's growth and expansion. Forbes had never been the kind of "boss" the books recommended; he had been austere, aloof, demanding, critical, and rather distant. But McAvoy had respected him and so had many others in Emitco. And Emitco's growth and success, McAvoy believed, was primarily the result of Forbes's management of people: he seemed to be able to make the most diverse people perform and pull together.

Forbes was at first cool when McAvoy sought him out in his retirement retreat in Colorado Springs. But he warmed when McAvoy explained why he had come. "That you worry, Tom, is in itself a very good sign," Forbes said, "and perhaps it's the only thing needed to make you do a good job. Managing people isn't that hard—if you know that it *is* your job and that it *is* work. The only thing that is truly important is . . ."

QUESTIONS

How would you finish the sentence? And what would you say to defend your choice of the one thing that is "truly important" in managing people? Would today's successful executives agree?

Case Number 19

How to Staff the Dead-end Job?

For a long time the worst labor relations in the retail business were those of one of the country's biggest department-store chains. Headquartered in the eastern United States, the chain had pioneered college recruiting in the late 1950s, amid great fanfare and a good deal of favorable publicity. By 1980 or so, it had become very apparent that not only had college recruiting not produced the desired crop of outstanding executives, it had produced truly horrible labor relations: there were strikes all the time, tremendous bitterness between management and employees, and a militant union that seemed determined to drive the company out of business altogether.

It was not difficult for a new human-resources director, hired to change what had become an intolerable situation, to figure out what had gone wrong—after half a dozen interviews with older employees, he had the answer. The college recruitment program had been started in the 1950s by the chain's first woman executive. Herself a graduate of one of the prestigious eastern women's colleges, a high government official in the late New Deal days, and chairwoman of the board of trustees of her alma mater, this personnel director had gone all out to provide jobs for women college graduates, and especially for graduates of the leading eastern women's schools, at a time when jobs for young women were scarce. She had sent recruiters to the campuses with instructions to look for the top students and especially for those who combined academic achievement with good looks. She then brought the women to company headquarters and put them through a three-day round of interviews with the top brass and a one-day "executive aptitude test." The "winners" were hired and put to work in the stockroom "to learn the business from the ground up." But since there were few promotional opportunities in retail selling—at least not above the level of sales associate—not many were ever promoted out of the stockroom, and even fewer were promoted beyond sales associate. Most of the women escaped through marriage, but that made the ones who stayed on all the more bitter, made them feel all the more betrayed.

The new human-resource director knew that he could not undo the damage, but he resolved not to continue to inflict it. He agreed that the stockroom job is the right place to begin in a department store, but at the same time, for most who work there, it is almost certain to be a dead-end job. There just aren't many available jobs on higher levels. He thought through what could be done and came up with three possible answers. One was to adjust hiring to the reality of the stockroom job. He could look for new employees with limited education and limited intelligence to whom a stockroom job would present a genuine challenge and the—rare—opportunity to be advanced to sales associate, a genuine opportunity. The second approach he proposed was to keep on recruiting bright and presentable top-ranking college graduates but to make sure that those for whom promotional opportunities could not be found within the company would be systematically placed in well-paid and attractive managerial jobs with other and especially smaller stores. Finally in his most radical proposal, he recommended changing the organization so that stockroom people would have responsibility for inventory control and for the merchandise displays in the store.

Every one of his proposals was immediately shot down by higher management. "All our department heads and buyers," top management said, "have started in the stockroom. Unless we hire the ablest and most promising beginners into the stockroom, we won't have any management ten or fifteen years from now. And to *place* people we have trained with the competition! That's unthinkable. And surely," top management said, "you can't be serious about giving stock clerks responsibility that properly belongs to store managers and buyers."

QUESTIONS

Can you think of any way in which to convince top management of the merits of each proposed alternative? Are there any others, by the way, that would make it possible to staff these dead-end jobs and yet provide the opportunity for achievement and satisfaction?

Case Number 20

The New Training Director in the Hospital

American hospitals are required by law to have a training director on staff to organize training for all employees other than physicians, who have their own training system. At first, training was confined to nurses. And the training director, while now supposed to direct the training of all groups, is still almost always an experienced senior nurse. In many hospitals, the training director has found the job difficult and frustrating. Even if there is money available, there usually isn't much time. And the other groups—X-ray technicians, medical technologists, physical therapists, social workers, psychiatric case workers, dieticians, and all the many groups who work in the office or in housekeeping and maintenance—tend to resent the interference of an "outsider" in their areas. It is, therefore, by no means uncommon for a training director to resign in total frustration.

And this is what happened twice in quick succession at Metropolitan Community Hospital.

Before the hospital administrator appointed a third training director, he thought it advisable to consult an expert in training at the local university. The administrator wanted a training program: what courses would the hospital organize, what methods should it employ, and how could it use existing training facilities in the area's colleges and universities? The training specialist listened politely for an hour and then said, "I don't know much about hospitals—only what I learned as a patient, and fortunately my experience as such is very limited. But I think I know enough about training to know that I wouldn't go about the job the way you propose to do it. Courses, methods, subject matter—all that comes last, if it comes at all. You have told me two important things. First, your hospital is extraordinarily complex—all these groups with different jobs, different backgrounds, and different needs. Second, you have at least three distinct areas in which people need to learn. They need to improve their technical skills on the job. They need to learn how to work with one another—nurses with X-ray people and dieticians, for instance. And they need to work on their skills and attitudes in caring for patients. Finally, you have told me that there is one big group for which you need not and should not do much in-house training—your clerical and business people. What they need, particularly in respect to job skills, is amply provided for through evening courses, seminars, and so on by colleges and by all kinds of management and professional societies. Your business manager should be expected to be your training director for clerical and business-office employees.

"But for the rest—and I gather that is three-quarters of your employment or more—I would suggest that you pick someone who sees this job as being a trainer of trainers and a training coordinator, rather than as being a training director. I imagine it will be a nurse. Nurses apparently are the only people in the hospital who see and know the entire hospital rather than just their own segment, and who are in daily working relationship with all the other groups as well as with patients and doctors. Tell your candidate to spend ninety days sitting down with small groups from each area, the department head, say, and a handful of employees, both a few experienced ones and a few young and green ones. Tell him or her to ask these groups where they see *their* learning needs. Where do they see opportunities to do the job better? What do they have to know, what do they have to learn? What information and knowledge do they need and what tools? Make sure that they think through each of the three dimensions of the hospital job separately—technical skills, organizational relationships within the hospital and between its groups, and patient care. And then ask your new training director to submit to you a statement of learning priorities for each area and each group—and then you, the training director, and the department heads together should work out a plan for in-hospital training. Then you'll find out what courses you need, where you want discussion groups, in what areas you are going to have each group have its own program—that'll probably be the case for most technical-skill areas, I imagine—and where you better bring together people from various departments and areas to learn from each other. Above all, emphasize to your training director and to your department heads that the training director's first job is not to be a trainer. It is to get other people to be trainers—nobody learns half as much as the person who is forced to teach. And what you are after isn't a big program and spending a lot of money. What you want is to create a climate of continuous learning throughout the whole hospital."

The hospital administrator was not impressed. "That's just common sense," he thought, "and I didn't need to consult a big expert for *that*."

QUESTIONS

But what do you think of the advice? Is it sensible? Is it realistic—the new training director, after all, is likely to be a novice at training no matter how good a nurse he or she might be.

And, assuming that the hospital administrator followed the advice, what kinds of things is the new training director likely to include in his or her priority list three months or six months hence?

Case Number 21

Are You One of "Us" or One of "Them"?

Labor relations at McDougal Machine Tools were considered exceptionally good by management as well as by the union. But socially "labor" and "management" kept apart from each other. Many of the workers were highly skilled craftsmen, and many made a good deal more money than first-line supervisors in the assembly plant or even the younger engineers and accountants. But no worker had, within living memory, been promoted out of the rank and file into a supervisory job, let alone into higher management. All supervisory jobs were staffed with engineering-school graduates who had been given a year's training under one of the plant superintendents and then served for another year or two as assistants before being appointed supervisor or staff engineer. Indeed, the two groups lived in different parts of town. And only at such occasions as the annual Christmas party did their families ever meet—and then they didn't mix. There was no hostility—on the job workers and supervisors used first names, joked together, helped each other, and clearly respected each other. But the two groups talked of each other as "us" and "them"—and because supervisory jobs tended to require substantial formal engineering knowledge, both groups, apparently, thought this relationship appropriate—the natural order of things.

Gregory Armitage, who had come into the plant as a young assembly-line worker and then had worked his way up to highly skilled tool setter, had no quarrel with the system—indeed, it made sense to him. But he was also an ambitious young man deeply interested in engineering. When, therefore, the local branch of the state university started an evening program in engineering, Gregory was one of the first to enroll. As it turned out, one of the plant's managers taught a course at the university and ran into Gregory at one of the first sessions. He beamed when he recognized one of his workers, and from then on he did everything to help Gregory continue his studies. It was he, for instance, who made sure that Gregory would not be given overtime assignments on evenings when his classes met. And he also made sure that Gregory got a full tuition refund from the company even though the tuition-refund plan, strictly speaking, applied to salaried personnel only.

When Gregory finally got his degree, he therefore called on the plant manager, who warmly congratulated him. But then Gregory said, "Now that I have an engineering degree, how do I apply for promotion to supervisor? I believe I am fully qualified."

"You are indeed," said the superintendent, "and yet I don't think it can work and I can't recommend you. We in management would welcome you. But I doubt that the men will accept you. You are one of them, and one of the younger ones to boot. They aren't going to accept you as one of us—not even if you move yourself and your family to the other side of town. The men will always wonder whether you are one of 'us' or one of 'them.' They'll resent you if you exercise a supervisor's authority, and they'll have no respect for you if you don't. I hate to say it, but I think you should try to get the supervisor's job you have earned someplace else, where you can start fresh—I'll gladly help you get it."

Gregory accepted the offer—he had little choice, after all. He soon found himself working as supervisor for another company, where he did well and became plant manager within a few years. But he also found that the plant manager had been right in predicting that he would have to move with his family. After a few months, his wife complained that she had no friends left in the old neighborhood. And he himself gradually drifted away from the many friends he had had among McDougal workers.

In other than blue-collar employment, the line between "them" and "us" in this country is quite a bit less pronounced than in the plant, but in most other countries it is equally sharp in the office or in the retail store.

QUESTIONS

Is such a line between "them" and "us" a good thing to have in a plant—or in a society? Could a management do anything to eliminate it in its own plants, or at least to make it a little less rigid?

Case Number 22

Midwest Metals and the Labor Union

Long before the mounting concern with health care and its cost explosion, Gene Kowalski, the president of the union local that represented most of Midwest Metals' hourly rated workers, called on the company's industrial relations vice president, Frank Snyder. "Our members," said Kowalski, "are increasingly unhappy with the medical and hospital care they receive under the company's plan. They feel that it is second-class care, and I have checked their complaints and agree with them. You'd better do something about it." "Gene," said the human-relations VP, "this is quite a coincidence. I have heard similar complaints from the supervisors and from our whole management group. At the same time that patient care under the plan is going down, costs are going up very fast; I have been pushed by top management to do something before they get out of control. And so, a few weeks ago, I asked our medical director, Dr. Furness, to look into the whole matter. Her report came in yesterday, and I was just going to call you to come over to discuss it with you. Dr. Furness thinks we ought to switch to a prepaid clinic plan, similar to the Kaiser Permanente Health Plan, which started in California. It's a plan with salaried doctors in a clinic and perhaps with its own hospital where one pays a fixed amount per person covered by the plan, rather than paying for services after they have been performed. Helen Furness recommends that we appoint a task force to study how best to do this, and what the advantages and disadvantages were."

Kowalski was enthusiastic. He had been about to propose a similar approach. But he refused to take the chairmanship of the task force that was offered to him. "Under our contract, health-care insurance is a management responsibility, and I can't participate in formulating a management plan." But he stayed close to the work of the task force. And he was in full agreement with its final recommendation to start a Midwest Medical Foundation that would have three clinics in the city, each staffed with twelve to fifteen salaried doctors, and owning its own small hospital—perhaps Park Street Hospital, which had an excellent plant but was in severe financial difficulties and was probably available for a moderate amount. Midwest Metals' ten thousand employees and their families would be barely enough to make such a plan work. But Dr. Furness, having checked with some of her colleagues in the city's other industries, felt confident that other major employers would soon join up also. The medical and hospital care offered by the new plan would be more comprehensive and better than the existing contract provided; yet, after a year or two there would probably be a substantial cost saving—as much as 40 percent. Still—on this Snyder was adamant—the company would continue to put aside the same amount of money as under the old plan. Any cost saving would go into a special fund for five years. Then it would be decided jointly by company and union whether the available savings should be used to improve the health-care plan (Snyder thought of including dental care or at least part of it) or for other employee benefits.

Kowalski was sure the plan would be welcomed by his members. "But, you know," he said to Snyder, "I can't accept a change in the contract; the executive committee of the local has to approve it and then submit it to the members for a vote. I don't foresee any trouble, though." He was wrong. When he presented the new plan to his executive committee, he was subjected to sharp questioning. "Does the new plan cost the company more or does it cost the company less?" was the persistent question. "It does cost less," said Kowalski, "but we'll get the savings anyhow." "Never mind who gets the savings," said his oldest and most respected executive-committee member. "What matters is that the company gains. And you can't convince me or anyone in the plant that it's a benefit to us if it costs the company less. We all know that the more it costs the company the better for us, and the less it costs the company the worse for us." And so the plan was voted down unanimously by the executive committee.

By now health-care costs have, of course, increased manyfold—but prepaid plans such as Dr. Furness proposed have at the same time lost some of their luster. And the union today would probably be willing to be a party to a task-force study, might even insist on it. The basic situation has not changed, however. Union members—and union leaders—do believe that the measurement of an employee benefit is not how much the workers benefit but how much it costs the company. And there are quite a few management people who agree with them, believing that the costs, rather than the benefits the costs produce, are the measurement of employee benefits.

QUESTIONS

What might explain this prevailing misconception? And what could be done to dispel it and to make possible a rational cost-benefit approach to employee benefits?

Case Number 23

Safety at Kajak Airbase

At the end of his first staff meeting, the new commandant of Kajak Tactical Airbase asked two of his officers to stay behind—his chief of operations and his chief safety inspector. "I know," he said, "that Kajak has the best safety record in Tactical Air Command. But I am not satisfied. I aim to run a base on which there are zero accidents."

"Sir," said the chief of operations, "we try—but fighter airplanes are inherently dangerous."

"They should be dangerous to the enemy," snapped the Commandant, "not to our men."

"We have three approaches," said the chief safety inspector, "and we might intensify all three of them. We study the equipment; of course, we have no control over design and manufacturing, but when we find something that might cause an accident—or find that something has caused one—we make sure that it is redesigned. We train and we train and we train. And when there is any mishap, even one that doesn't injure anyone, we have a thorough inquiry and, if necessary, change the method of operations or the equipment and, of course, recommend appropriate punishment if the mishap is the result of sloppy or careless operations. We can intensify our work—I, for one, have always asked for more training time—but I doubt that we'll get a great deal out of more intensive efforts. This is already the most safety-conscious base I know."

The commandant was not impressed, however, and asked both men to come up with specific proposals—and he repeated his intention to run a base with zero accidents. After a week, the two officers reported.

"I'd suggest a permanent safety competition," said the chief of operations, "as one approach. Post on the bulletin boards the names of the units that have no accidents in a month; recognize their performance; reward them—a few extra passes often do wonders; and make it clear that recommendation or promotion goes to officers and noncommissioned officers [NCOs] who stand out in the safety competition. At the same time," continued the chief of operations, "we might borrow from industry. I have few friends at General Motors who tell me that they run plants with zero accidents by relieving from responsibility, pending investigation, any supervisor who has even the slightest accident, even if there is no injury; and they also relieve his boss until the inquiry is concluded. If the supervisor has a second accident within a twelve-month period, they remove him and demote his boss. The only excuse is equipment failure over which the supervisor had no control."

"Not bad," said the commandant, "although I'd have to go upstairs to get authority to remove or demote people—but perhaps there is some other way to accomplish the same end."

"Sir," said the chief safety inspector, "I am impressed by my colleague's ideas and think we might try them. But I have three other proposals. One, we might systematically encourage accident-anticipation reports. We have a suggestion system that includes suggestions on safe operations—and it works well. But we might ask each commander and each supervisor to give us a monthly report on everything within his authority that might pose even the slightest potential safety hazard—whether equipment, operations, or the way we staff or train. My second possible suggestion would be for regular monthly safety meetings in each area of the base devoted to the question, What can each of us do to make the work totally safe? And—my third suggestion—we might have one presentation at each of these meetings in which one commander or supervisor reports on what methods he has found effective in making his operation accident-proof."

"Do you think you could do these things without running up costs to the point where we get Washington on our back, and without impairing the combat effectiveness of the Command?" asked the commandant.

Both men thought it could be done—or at least there was enough probability to try each approach experimentally in a part of the base.

QUESTIONS

What do you think of these five proposals? What principles in managing people does each represent? How likely is each to have an impact? Which are likely to be welcomed by the personnel on the base? Are any likely to be resisted? What does each assume about the causes of accidents?

Part V

Social Impacts and Social Responsibilities

Case Number 24

Corporate Image to Brand Image: Yuhan-Kimberly*

PETER PARKER: Whatever life holds in store for me, I will never forget these words: "With great power comes great responsibility." This is my gift, my curse. Who am I? I'm Spider-Man.

Columbia Pictures movie, *Spider-Man*

Kook-Hyun Moon, CEO of Yuhan-Kimberly in Seoul, Korea, is emphatic in his belief that private-sector organizations hold *great power* in capitalist societies and with great power comes *great responsibility.* Mr. Moon argues that a social campaign or movement cannot be conducted by an individual, but must be conducted by organizations that hold great power.

Since 1984, Yuhan-Kimberly has been involved in an environmental movement, a movement that has come to be known as Keep Korea Green. The Keep Korea Green movement at Yuhan-Kimberly is a result of the power of a successful private-sector corporation and its felt responsibility toward the environment. Yuhan-Kimberly (Y-K)

* This case was prepared by Min S. Shin of the Peter F. Drucker and Masatoshi Ito Graduate School of Management under the supervision of Professor Joseph A. Macciariello. Materials were provided by Mr. Kook-Hyun Moon, President and Chief Executive Officer of Yuhan-Kimberly, Limited, January 2008.

also believes that fulfilling social responsibility is directly related to creating customers, a true purpose of a private-sector organization.

KEEP KOREA GREEN

Figure 24.1

Keep Korea Green logo

For example, Y-K's movement, Keep Korea Green, has as its objective to improve the quality of the environment by restoration of the forest (i.e., reforestation). Y-K established a fund to form a committee of industry experts and scholars in forestry to promote forest restoration. Y-K offered corporate-sponsored and educational opportunities for young people and newly wed couples in areas such as planting trees, cultivating forests, and protecting young trees in the national forests. Since 1996, Y-K has also sponsored environmental research that supported publication of forty-three academic studies on environmental protection. In a third initiative to protect the environment of the Korean peninsula, Y-K began a project in 1999 to assist forest restoration in North Korea, as shown in Table 24.1.

Table 24.1

Year	1999	2000	2001–2002	2003	2004	2005	2006	2007
Number of trees	2,167,830	130,000	211,750	30,115	131,096	203,804	10,000	6,000

Trees planted in North Korea

FROM CORPORATE IMAGE TO BRAND IMAGE

Y-K's dominant position in the female sanitary napkin market in South Korea started to erode in 1993 when Procter & Gamble (P&G) entered the market in South Korea. The absorbent capacity and slim design of P&G's *Whisper* led retailers to devote less shelf-space to Y-K products. In order to differentiate their product from *Whisper*, Y-K developed a new product, *White*, with a marketing theme that emphasized a clean break from the unsanitary image associated with female menstruation. This clean-image marketing was successful in creating customers, and Y-K retrieved its market dominance by 1999.

Mr. Moon credits the success of *White* to its association by consumers with the clean image established by Y-K as an environment-friendly organization, through its Keep Korea Green movement.

QUESTIONS

Drucker argues that organizations should seek first to achieve their primary mission. Is forest restoration directly related to Y-K's business? If not, how can it be justified?

Case Number 25

The Peerless Starch Company of Blair, Indiana

For as long as anyone in Blair, Indiana, could remember, the Peerless Starch plant had always been the biggest thing in town. Built on a slight hill above the sluggish river, and designed to look as much like the Tower of London as anything in Indiana can, the plant dominated the town spiritually even more than it did physically.

Peerless was the largest employer in town, employing well over 8,000 men out of a population of 120,000—or every fourth head of a family. It paid the highest wages, if only because most of the men were rated as skilled workers or technicians. And alone of all the large businesses in Blair, it was locally managed; the Peerless top management sat on the fifth floor of the big mill itself, in the "New Building" that had been put up in the 1940s. And from the chief executive officer—the grandson of the founder—on down, all executives were Blair men who had started in the mill and worked their way up, and who were more often than not second- or third-generation Peerless employees.

Peerless had started in Blair during the Civil War when the founder had developed one of the first methods to extract starch from corn. Until the 1940s, Peerless had only one mill. But the company had prospered so much that three additional mills were built in rapid succession during the years after World War II: one in Illinois, one in Texas, and, the biggest yet, in Oregon, built in the late 1950s.

But while Peerless had flourished, the town of Blair had not. During World War II it had boomed. But then Blair had gradually drifted into being first a run-down and then a depressed area. One after the other of the town's factories had laid off people and then finally closed its doors. The Peerless mill in Blair seemed to be the only exception to this general rule of slow decay and downhill drift. But appearances were deceptive. Actually, the Peerless mill in Blair was in dire straits and was kept going only by the success of the new mills in other states.

Blair's sales were about one-fifth of the entire Peerless Company's. But the Blair Mill employed almost half of Peerless's hourly rated labor force and three-quarters of Peerless's managerial and professional people. Unlike the other mills, Blair did not make its own raw materials but got intermediates from outside suppliers or from the other mills. It should, therefore, have needed less labor per unit produced. Instead, it needed up to four times as much.

There were reasons for Blair's high costs—or at least there were arguments to justify them. The mill itself was a towering structure built to withstand the Crusaders' armies but ill-equipped for modern production. All newer Peerless mills, for instance, were single-story buildings, whereas Blair had five stories capped by twin towers. Nobody at Blair ever got fired; if a man couldn't do a job, the word from the head office was "Find him another one." If a new process came in, the workers on the old one were quietly moved to plant maintenance—or, if they had any skills, were made supervisors, with the ludicrous result that there were whole departments with more supervisors than workers. Above all, Blair considered itself a "quality mill," and that apparently meant that nothing could be produced in quantity. But the central problem of Blair—and the greatest drain in money—was precisely that Blair did *not* turn out quality products. Rejection rates at Blair ran almost twice as high as at the other mills. What the Blair quality-control inspectors accepted provoked angry complaints from the customers. Indeed, as everyone knew, the sales-people spent little time selling. They spent most of their time talking customers into not sending the stuff right back to Blair as faulty and unusable—often by granting the complaining customer a nice rebate. It never appeared in the Blair direct cost accounts but was charged off to the overhead account "miscellaneous customer service."

Things had been drifting from bad to worse—and no one in Blair expected that they would ever change. But then suddenly, in the spring of 1985, a number of circumstances coalesced.

1. The founder's grandson, the "old man" who had run Peerless for thirty-five years, died. And it turned out that the founding family owned practically no stock at all. Thereupon the outside directors, who had not dared speak up while the "old man" was alive, refused to appoint his son-in-law or his nephew as his successor. Instead they picked an outsider to become president and chief executive officer: John Ludwig, who was not even a native of Blair, let alone a chemical engineer or a starch machinist. In fact, Ludwig had been with Peerless less than four years—and had been imposed on the "old man" by some of the outside directors. Having started as an industrial psychologist, Ludwig had first taught, then worked for the Pentagon as a training specialist, then in Industrial Relations for Ford, where he helped reorganize one of the major divisions and then had become general manager of one of the smaller Ford Motor divisions. He had come to Peerless in 1981 as its first "professional manager"—at least the first one in Blair—and as executive assistant to the president. The "old man" had kept him busy with the affairs of the other plants, so that he knew very little about Blair. Although he had several times thought of resigning what he felt was a futile and frustrating assign-ment, he now found himself in charge.

2. Even before the death of the "old man," things had turned critical at Peerless, and especially at Blair. The market had sud-denly become competitive. Synthetic starches and adhesives were flowing onto the market out of the labs of the chemical companies and the oil companies and the rubber companies—businesses that

never before had been competing in the starch market. Peerless and a few other companies used to have the field all to themselves—and carefully refrained from hurting each other too badly. But the newcomers didn't know what everyone else in the industry knew: you can't make the market bigger by lowering the price or improving product performance; all you can do is spoil the market for everybody. Worse still, the success of the newcomers seemed to disprove such old "truths."

3. The new mills in Illinois, Texas, and Oregon had managed to hold their own—indeed Oregon did phenomenally well and managed to bring out a highly profitable new line of synthetics (without even telling the folks in Central Research in Blair) that quickly became industry leaders. But Blair came close to collapse. With supply abundant, customers flatly refused to tolerate the Blair quality—or lack of quality—anymore. Despite all the efforts of the sales department, whole carloads of the stuff came back—often with a curt note: "Don't bother to call on us anymore; we have contracted to buy our supply elsewhere." And Blair, which for years had been barely breaking even, plunged into the red. By mid-1985 Blair was losing more money than the other three mills made, so that Peerless no longer showed any profit and, indeed, barely managed to earn the interest on its fixed debt. Blair, clearly, was bleeding Peerless white.

As soon as Ludwig had become president, he asked the ablest man in Blair management—an assistant manager of the Blair plant—to study what could be done with Blair. The result was a recommendation to spend some $25 million on modernizing the Blair plant. For this sum, the assistant manager promised, Peerless would get as modern a plant as any in the country (to build one from scratch would cost around $60 million). Employment in the modernized plant would shrink from 8,000 to 2,600.

Ludwig had resolved not to take any action until the assistant manager completed his study. But he hadn't been idle during that time. He himself carefully studied the economics of Peerless, which had previously been kept rather secret. It soon became apparent to Ludwig that, economically, Blair was untenable. The only economically justifiable course was to close the Blair mill and not replace it. The existing mills in Illinois, Texas, and Oregon could easily replace Blair's production volume—at a fraction of Blair's cost and at superior quality. Closing Blair would entail very heavy short-run costs, mainly severance pay. But within six months, the Peerless Company would have absorbed the loss and would have become profitable again. If Blair was kept going, no matter how successfully modernized, Peerless could at best hope to break even—and the capital required to rebuild Blair would use up all the credit Peerless could possibly command—if indeed that much money could be raised in Peerless's shaky condition.

Ludwig was deeply disturbed by this conclusion. He knew how much the Peerless Mill meant to Blair; without it there weren't going to be any jobs in the town. He himself was old enough to remember the Depression days when his father, a machinist in a Milwaukee automobile plant, had been unemployed for three bitter years. Yet Ludwig also knew that he had to make a decision fast. When he had been made president, he had asked the board of directors to give him six months to study the situation—and the board had given him that much time only grudgingly. At that time the board had not really known how bad things were—and at the next Board meeting, in January 1986, he would have to tell them that the first nine months of 1985 had been catastrophic months. Surely at that meeting, if not before, the board would expect him to have a definite recommendation.

As a business decision, there was clearly no choice: Blair had to be closed. But what about the company's social responsibility to Blair and to the people who depended on the Peerless mill for their livelihood? The more Ludwig thought about this the more he became convinced that Peerless had the social responsibility to try to save the Blair mill, and the town with it. There was a fair chance, after all, that the rescue operation would succeed. He was not at all sure that his board would go along—indeed, he half-suspected that the board would ask for his resignation rather than authorize spending $25 million on Blair. Still he saw no choice in conscience but to try. But before recommending to the board that the Blair mill be remodeled, Ludwig thought it prudent to discuss the matter with an old acquaintance, Glen Baxter. Baxter had attended the same college as Ludwig, had wanted to become a minister, and had actually had a year or two of divinity school, but had then turned to economics and was now the economist for the very union that represented the Peerless workers. Ludwig was really more interested in getting Baxter's support than in getting his advice—privately, he had always considered Baxter somewhat of a "radical" and an "oddball." But Ludwig knew that he needed union support for any plan to rebuild Blair—and that his board would not even listen to such a plan unless he could give assurances of union support. And surely Baxter would support a plan that maintained 2,600 jobs for his members!

Much to Ludwig's surprise, Baxter did no such thing. On the contrary, he became almost violent in his opposition. "To invest all this money in rebuilding Blair," he said, "is not only financial folly; it's totally irresponsible socially. You aren't just president of the Blair mill; you are president of the Peerless Company with its 8,000 employees outside of Blair. And you propose to sacrifice the 8,000 people you employ outside of Blair to the people at Blair. You have no right to do so. Even if you succeed and Blair survives, Peerless will have lost the capacity both to pay severance pay and pensions should you have to lay off more people and to raise the money to modernize and expand the other mills and to maintain the jobs there. All right, John Ludwig, maybe you'll be a hero in Blair with your plan, maybe people there will think you've done great things for them. But in my book you'll be a cheap demagogue—as president of the company you are paid for doing the right thing and not for being popular."

"Of course," Baxter said, "we in the union will do everything to make closing Blair as expensive as possible for Peerless—we do have a responsibility toward our members. But for you to jeopardize the jobs and livelihoods of the workers in the healthy plants just because you have a guilty conscience about Blair's mismanagement all these years—that's the height of social irresponsibility."

QUESTIONS

Does Baxter have a case? Would today's successful executives agree?

Part VI

The Manager's Work and Jobs

Case Number 26

Alfred Sloan's Management Style

Rarely has a chief executive of an American corporation been as respected and as revered as Alfred P. Sloan, Jr., was at General Motors during his long tenure at the top—from 1920 until 1955. Many GM managers, especially those who grew up in the 1920s and 1930s, felt a deep personal gratitude to him for his quiet but decisive acts of kindness, of help, of advice, or just of warm sympathy when they were in trouble. At the same time, however, Sloan kept aloof from the entire managerial group in GM. That he never called anyone by his or her first name and was "Mr. Sloan" even to top executives may have been a reflection of his generation and upbringing—he had been born, after all, in the 1870s and was a senior executive, running his own business, before 1900. However, unlike most of his generation, he also addressed the African-American elevator men in the GM building in Detroit or New York in the same way. They were always "Mr. Smith" or "Mr. Jones." When he met a new elevator attendant, he would introduce himself, "I am Mr. Sloan. What is your name?" When the man answered, "I am Jack, sir," Sloan would turn white with anger and would say, "I asked for your name, sir,"—and would from then on always remember it. Sloan also frowned on the use of first names by his top people among themselves. It was known, for instance, that he felt it unwise of Mr. Wilson—for many years GM's president and later Sloan's successor as chief executive officer—that he was on first-name terms with most of GM's vice presidents.

Above all, Sloan had no friends within the GM group. He was a warm and had been a gregarious man until deafness cut him off from easy human contact. Although he had had close friends, he outlived them all—he lived well into his nineties. All these friends had been outside General Motors. Indeed, the one friend who had been in GM, Walter P. Chrysler, did not become a personal friend until after he had left GM and had, upon Sloan's advice and with strong support from Sloan, started his own competing automobile company.

As Sloan grew older, he keenly felt his increasing isolation as his close friends died one by one. Yet he remained aloof from GM people. He never invited them to his home. Unless it was a business meeting with a clear business agenda, he did not even sit down to a meal with any of them. He never accepted an invitation to any of their homes, even on business trips to their hometowns. He was once asked how he liked Winterthur, the estate of Henry Francis du Pont, a cousin of Pierre S. du Pont, who had been his boss at GM in 1919 and 1920 and chairman of the GM board for years thereafter. "I have never been to any of the du Pont homes," he answered. "Ours is a business relationship." In his earlier years, Sloan had been a keen outdoorsman—but his hiking, fishing, and camping companions had all been non-GM people. Only after his retirement in 1955, when advancing old age made it more and more difficult for him to travel, did he invite GM people to come to his home in New York—and then only to discuss business in the office wing of his apartment—for he was still a GM director and a member of the top committees.

"It is the duty of the chief executive officer to be objective and impartial," Sloan said, explaining his management style. "He must be absolutely tolerant and pay no attention to how a man does his work, let alone whether he likes a man or not. The only criteria must be performance and character. And that is incompatible with friendship and social relations. A chief executive officer, who has 'friendships' within the company, has 'social relations' with colleagues or discusses anything with them except the job, cannot remain impartial—or at least, which is equally damaging, he will not appear as such. Loneliness, distance, and formality may be contrary to his temperament—they have always been contrary to mine—but they are his duty."

QUESTIONS

What do you think of this? And would such successful chief executives as Abraham Lincoln or Franklin D. Roosevelt have agreed? Would today's successful executives agree?

Case Number 27

Performance Development System at Lincoln Electric for Service and Knowledge Workers*

A management-consulting firm was engaged by the Lincoln Electric Company during 1996 to review the use of a merit rating system for all *hourly* and *salaried nonproduction personnel*. The consultant conducted focus-group meetings with employees who had previously expressed some dissatisfaction with the way they were being evaluated and rewarded. The result of these focus-group meetings led to recommendations to management that a new merit rating system be developed for nonproduction employees.

As a result of this study, a new system called the *Performance Development System* (PDS) was introduced at Lincoln Electric in late 1997, preceded by three months of training that was conducted by representatives of the Human Resources Department. The PDS is applied to all salaried and hourly nonproduction employees and to the managers of these employees.

Four steps made up the Performance Development System:

---

* This case was prepared from information contained in Joseph A. Maciariello's *Lasting Value*, John Wiley & Sons, New York, New York, 1999

1. Performance planning

2. Performance coaching

3. Interim review

4. Performance evaluation and rating.

These four steps are used to plan work and evaluate work and to develop the human resources of the company. The PDS is applied to employees in sales, engineering, information technology, human resources, and plant maintenance and in office support functions.

An overview of the Performance Development System is contained in figure 27.1. Lincoln's strategic business plan is used to guide operations of the PDS. This strategic business plan is the reference point for all of the planning, evaluation, and development that takes place within the PDS.

Figure 27.1

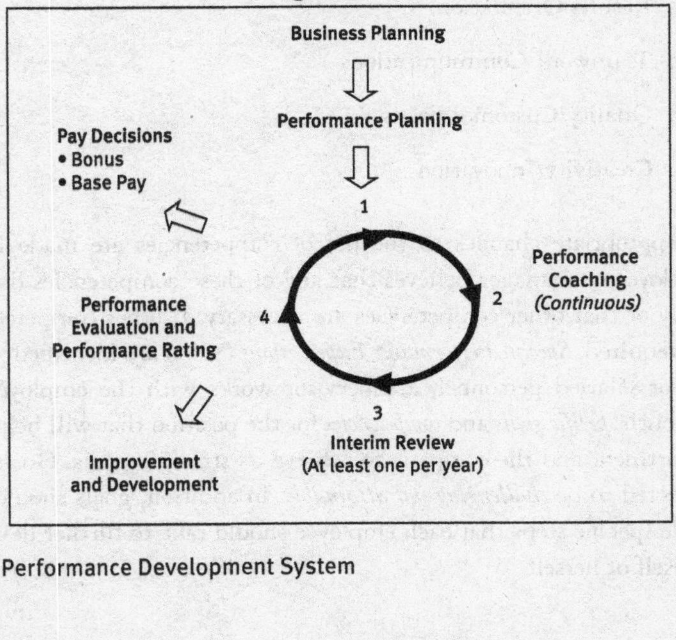

The Performance Development System

The PDS begins with employee *performance planning*. Each manager shares the content of the overall business plan with each employee as it relates to the function of the employee. This then becomes the basis for each individual's annual performance planning process. The manager works in consultation with each employee to develop a performance plan for the next year, but the ultimate approval of the plan rests with the supervisor.

The difference between the ingredients of a performance plan for hourly and salaried personnel is that for hourly personnel the emphasis in the PDS is to identify the *competencies* that are critical to the performance of a particular position given the needs of the department and the company. The six general competencies applied to all employees are

1. Leadership/Ownership

2. Decision Making/Judgment

3. Results Orientation

4. Teamwork/Communications

5. Quality/Customer Focus

6. Creativity/Innovation

Appropriate changes to the list of competencies are made if an employee or manager believes that any of these competencies do not apply or that other competencies are necessary. If other competencies are required, *Specific Performance Expectations* (SPEs) are identified.

For salaried personnel, a supervisor works with the employee to establish *specific goals* and *competencies* for the position that will help the department and the company to achieve its strategic goals. Goals are expected to be *challenging but attainable*. In addition, goals should include specific steps that each employee should take to further develop himself or herself.

Goals are expected to be specific, measurable, attainable, relevant, and time-based. These five specifications for goals form the acronym SMART. They are self-explanatory except to note that a goal may be measured either quantitatively or qualitatively.

Once goals and competencies are formulated for salaried employees, each is weighted according to the priorities of the department and company. For salaried employees, goals and competencies must total 100 points. Goals must range from 40 to 60 points and competencies must range from 40 to 60 points. No single competency should be assigned more than 20 points. Only competencies, not goals, are developed for hourly employees. And, as in the case of salaried employees, the weightings must equal 100 points but no competency should exceed 30 points.

Once performance planning is complete, *performance coaching* begins. Performance coaching is an ongoing process throughout the year of providing employees help in meeting their performance objectives. In this process employees are expected to get feedback and receive recognition from supervisors. Employees may seek help in removing any impediments to achieving their objectives. Progress is noted, as are problems. This is both a formal and an informal review process. Employees are encouraged to continuously self-assess their progress during the year against their performance objectives.

The third step in the PDS is the *interim review*. Each employee meets with his or her supervisor at least once during the year. At this point there is a discussion of progress toward building competencies and achieving goals. A discussion then ensues about the employee's annual performance evaluation. Next, steps for improving performance and competencies during the following period are discussed.

This leads to the final step in the annual PDS process, *performance evaluation and rating*. A formal meeting is held once a year by each supervisor to discuss and assess the progress employees have made in improving skills, developing themselves, and achieving their objectives. This in turn leads the manager to rate each employee according to five criteria.

Criteria for Performance Rating

1. Exceeds expectations　　　　1.2

2. Meets all expectations　　　　1.0

3. Meets most expectations　　　0.8

4. Meets some expectations　　　0.6

5. Does not meet expectations　0.2

The point value assigned to each competency and objective is then multiplied by the appropriate performance rating that applies. The number of points for each competency and objective are totaled. Points for *all* competencies and objectives are then totaled. Total points are then used to make adjustments to base wages and salaries and become part of the formula for determining bonuses.

The total number of points for a department under the PDS may not average 100 per employee. To remedy this situation, total performance ratings are adjusted proportionately so that PDS ratings will average 100 points per employee.

Nonproduction employees who are rated over 110 points are eligible for superior rewards. Points in excess of 110 are added to the total points of the department so as not to take these extra points away from other employees within the department. In this way, superior performance is rewarded and other employees are not penalized. Approval of senior management is required before any employee can be rated over 110 points.

In the words of the manager of Human Resources, "The goal of the performance planning, development, and evaluation system is to bring alignment between the interests of Lincoln Electric and those of its employees. Its purpose is to provide value to customers, employees, and stockholders. It seeks to distribute the rewards of the firm justly to those who produce the output."

QUESTIONS

How similar is the PDS to "management by objectives and self-control"? Does a system like the PDS have the potential to create the alignment spoken of by the manager of Human Resources? Does the PDS help to create conditions under which leaders may emerge? What are the limitations of the PDS? Would the PDS work in your organization? Why or why not?

Case Number 28

Internal and External Goal Alignment at Texas Instruments*

In 1995 and for some time after, Texas Instruments (TI) and a number of other organizations, such as AT&T, Raytheon, and the U.S. Air Force, began using the "catchball" process for seeking (internal) goal alignment within their organizations.** During this same time, Texas Instruments also experienced exceptional success in achieving (external) goal alignment on some of its interorganizational teams. This case explores both of these goal-alignment processes.

Catchball starts with overarching goals—a big idealistic vision, which the company promotes in all of their internal communications. Everybody knows these overarching goals. At first people look at them and say, "Okay, but I don't fit there. I don't see myself being networked into [say] the TI world. I solder circuit boards. How do I fit?"

In response, TI's top executives gathered literally hundreds of supervisors over days and weeks and communicated these goals. Each

---

* Information on TI's catchball process and on the Joint Standoff Weapon System was obtained from a research project carried out by Dr. Karen L. Higgins and is reported in Karen L. Higgins and Joseph A. Maciariello's "Leading Complex Collaboration in Network Organizations: A Multidisciplinary Approach," *Advances in Interdisciplinary Studies of Work Teams*, vol. 10, pp. 203–241. It is used by permission of Dr. Karen L. Higgins.

** Baldridgeplus.com, Exhibit, "Catchball Processes." http://www.baldridgeplus.com/Exhibits/Exhibit%20-%20Catchball%20processes.pdf (accessed December 20, 2007).

of these supervisors went back and said, "This is how my organization fits." It was like throwing a ball: "Here you go; here are the goals, what are you going to do with them?" "I caught them. Now I'm going to share them with my people or with the next supervisory level down. Okay, here you go. What does it mean to your particular organization?"

Interviews at TI demonstrated that people at all levels knew the overarching goals. Furthermore, they knew their contribution to those goals. They were committed to these goals because they knew the goals. They accepted the goals. They trusted that the organization was concerned about the goals and that the goals were for their benefit. As a result, they were highly motivated to accomplish their goals.

So, this process of communication became extremely important. And the way TI did it was very effective, because they involved everyone. Everyone had to write down in his or her own performance plan: "This is what I'm going to do, and this is how it fits." The catchball process at TI illustrates an exemplary goal-alignment process for an organization and its individuals.

At about the same time, many of TI's interorganizational teams were achieving only modest success in attaining goal alignment among the participants of different organizations. One of TI's interorganizational teams, the Joint Standoff Weapon System Program, however, was very effective in the way it managed these interorganizational relations.

This team comprised a number of organizations working on the project. TI, of course, was one of them. The federal government was one of them, including government personnel from all over the country. The team also included multiple suppliers and other specialists.

The two major leaders on the interorganizational team, TI and the government, started the project by telling all team partners, "We will spend time in team building because we believe it is critical to a successful project. This project is highly important, so we have to establish trust on our team, determine and align goals, gain pride in our goals, and finally, commit to our goals."

Team members spent days together, and many complained saying, "Why are you wasting this time? Let's just get on with it." But they spent days working on these issues. They worked at understanding what the project was all about: What were the project goals? How were they going to operate? And how were they going to resolve conflicts?

Whenever a team member came to one organization to complain about someone from another organization, executives would say, "Stop, we do not want to hear this. You work it out because we are all working together. We are working on the same goal and the goal is . . ." The leadership continued to make these very clear statements regarding what the team was about. As a result, there was no problem understanding what project goals were, or how the team was going to operate, or understanding that leaders would not tolerate adversarial relationships on the team.

The leadership on this team—and it was a system of leaders—was saying, "We are working together. We have linked arms and we won't tolerate any kind of negative behavior." And they didn't. The result was the strongest, most successful interorganizational team at TI, as witnessed by an independent researcher.

Top leaders took the time to establish the ground rules and to set the team in place. Then they empowered people, saying: "These are our values." "These are our goals." "This is how we will work together." So, the integrity, the abilities, the characteristics, of the leadership group filtered into the rest of the team and extraordinary performance resulted.

QUESTIONS

1. *What are the strengths and limitations of the catchball process for achieving organizational alignment?*

2. *Using your knowledge of management by objectives, comment on the following analysis of the catchball process by Gary Siegel, of DePaul University:*

    Ideas generated at one level of an organization are passed up or down to people at other organization levels. Those receiving the idea *"catch" it, modify it so that it is relevant to the work done at their level, and pass it along to another level. This is called* catchball. *A major benefit of catchball is that it helps to vertically integrate an organization. Communication is enhanced, people participate in developing ideas, and when the ideas are implemented, the chances of success are high because people at all levels in the organization shaped it so that it would work best in their environment. Each person will know how his or her work relates to the strategic and tactical operation of the business . . . [and] crossfunctional teams work better if the organization is first vertically integrated.* *

3. *What requirements for effective management of the "systems organization" are illustrated by the management of the Joint Standoff Weapon System Program?*

4. *What principles of managing alliances are illustrated by the management of the Joint Standoff Weapon System Program?*

---

* http://www.baldridgeplus.com/Exhibits/Exhibit%20%20Catchball%20processes.pdf (page 3, accessed January 16, 2008).

Case Number 29

Can You Manage Your Boss?

After four years of working under Pete Webster, Larry Frankenmuth had had it. The work itself was fine—he was in charge of the company's four metalworking plants, knew the work, liked it, and was sure he did a good job. His subordinates were great. Every one of the four plant managers was first-rate, easy to work with, competent, on top of his job. The company was fine and clearly going places. The pay was good.

But *Webster!* Webster was a pain in every part of Larry's body from top to toe. Never an encouraging word, only grunts or criticism. Larry slaved on the memoranda and reports he sent up to Webster's office— and then he never heard anything about them. He always made sure to be in Webster's office first thing in the morning with anything important—or to call him at 8:30 sharp. His first boss had drilled that into him when Larry started as a manufacturing engineer. Yet Webster always acted as if Larry had broken all Ten Commandments when he knocked at the door and asked whether he could come in. "What have you to see me about *again*, Frankenmuth?" he'd growl. But he'd also bite his head off if Larry did not tell him to the last detail every single thing that was going on, and especially any bad news ahead. But the worst thing about Webster was his appalling illiteracy. Larry Frankenmuth—with a BA and an MA in mechanical engineering from MIT—had then, on his own time, gone and taken all the courses he could get in modern management, in modern production, in operations research, and in quantitative methods. Then to have to work for a boss who hadn't finished high school! Webster had gone into the army at the end of his junior year in high school and then started as a machinist when he came back from the service. He probably couldn't even do long division and surely could not follow the simplest regression analysis. It was too much!

And so Larry Frankenmuth decided to leave. He realized that he had made the right decision on a Sunday evening when he had worked at home on a careful study of order patterns and production schedules that added up to a recommendation to change production scheduling, inventory control, and shipping schedules for all four plants of the metalworking division. It was the most searching analysis he had yet made, and he felt very good about it. But as he was about to put the pages together for the following morning, he suddenly realized that there was absolutely no point in showing the work to Webster. "The old coot just couldn't understand," he said to himself. "And if he could, he'd still be much too reactionary to make any change in what has been procedure since before I was born. He'll never even read the report, I bet. And instead of discussing the figures, he'll treat me to one of his endless anecdotes about the good old days. I just can't take any more of it."

And so without even telling his wife, Lois, he set about finding another job. He had little difficulty in finding one. The new job was not quite as big, not quite as well paid, and with a company that had only limited growth opportunities, but the company was a highly technological one, and so Larry's management science was fully appreciated. Indeed, Larry was now the one who felt somewhat undereducated, since so many of his new associates had PhDs. Lois approved: she had long known how frustrated Larry had been. Webster approved in his boorish fashion. When Larry went in to tell him, he only said, "I won't try at talk you out of it. I have to tell you, Frankenmuth, that I could not and would not have recommended you for a promotion. Your leaving makes it much easier for all of us." And so Larry packed his papers and prepared to move out of the office in which he had suffered for four long years.

Two days before he left, he had an unexpected visitor: Frank Sartorius, the plant manager who was to take Larry's job. Sartorius's selection had surprised Larry. Larry had been sure Webster would pick the oldest and most conventional of his four plant managers. Instead he chose the youngest—Sartorius was well under forty—the most innovative, the boldest. In fact, Larry had to admit to himself that he would have hesitated to take the gamble. Sartorius had been plant manager for only a few years, and Larry doubted whether he was really ready yet. Larry had gotten along fairly well with Sartorius, but did not consider himself close to the man. Larry was therefore somewhat surprised when Sartorius called up, said that he was coming to the headquarters city in a day or two, and would like a private, off-the-record session at Larry's home. He was even more surprised when Sartorius said, "Larry, I was quite shocked when I heard that you were leaving. I was even more shocked when Webster called me and told me I'd take over from you. I didn't expect a big promotion for another three, four years, if then. What can you tell me that will help me?"

Larry spent an hour or two discussing the plants and their managers, and another hour talking about the relationships and problems inside the company—in particular about a long-standing feud with Purchasing and about the rather prickly Personnel Department and its failure to back operating management against the union. Finally he said, "Frank, I guess you know most of this." And Frank Sartorius nodded. "But," continued Larry, "the really important thing about this job isn't the plants, it isn't Purchasing or Personnel or the accountants. It is that impossible SOB, the boss. He doesn't read a line—you might as well write on water. He never has a word of praise, never, but is quick to criticize. He expects you to keep him informed about everything and is positively indecent in his insistence that you inform him ahead of time of anything unexpected. Yet he bites your head off when you come in to tell him. He is such an old reactionary that you just don't dare propose any change. You'll have no real trouble with any part of your job—it's in good shape, and the men are a pleasure to work with—but you just won't be able to manage the boss."

Larry Frankenmuth soon forgot all about his old company—the new job turned out to be a great deal tougher than he had expected and kept him fully occupied. He once ran into old Webster at the airport and asked him how Sartorius was doing—only to get a gruff "Why should I tell you?" for an answer. So he was quite surprised to read three years later, in *The Wall Street Journal*, that Frank Sartorius had been appointed to succeed Pete Webster as manufacturing vice president when Webster moved up to executive vice president in charge of the metalworking and mechanical divisions. "I must send Sartorius a note of congratulations when I get home tonight," he said to himself. But when he got back home he found that Sartorius had anticipated him. On the hall table was a huge flowerpot with a hand-written note from Sartorius.

Dear Larry Frankenmuth:
   You will have heard that I have been promoted to VP-Manufac-turing—and I owe it all to you and want to say "Thank You." You have taught me that I had to learn to manage the boss. And you told me how to do it.

                                        Cordially,
                                        Frank Sartorius

QUESTIONS

Can you tell the dumbfounded Larry Frankenmuth what Sartorius meant? And what did Larry tell Sartorius about managing that tough, reactionary SOB of a boss, Pete Webster?

Case Number 30

Ross Abernathy and the Frontier National Bank

The Frontier National Bank was the oldest bank in one of the country's rapidly growing regions. For many years it had also been the region's biggest and most profitable bank. But beginning around the time of the Vietnam War it had become increasingly stodgy—at Frontier they preferred to call it conservative—and had steadily lost market standing and, beginning around 1985, profitability. By the late 1980s, it had slipped to third place in assets in its region, and to sixth place in profits. It was still one of the nation's best-known banks and, with about $7 billion in assets, still a very big bank. But it did mainly routine business with traditional customers. This it accomplished with an enormous staff—almost twice as many employees per dollar of assets as the number one bank in the region—and at a snail's pace.

In 1994, the bank was still headed by a member of the founding family—the founder's great-grandson. The family no longer held any stock worth speaking of, but the bank still spoke reverently of the family. So, when the head man reached age seventy, the bank's retirement age, he proposed, as a matter of course, that his son-in-law succeed him. To his—and everybody else's—surprise, the board of directors balked. Indeed, during the preceding year, with the "old man's" retirement imminent, the comptroller of the currency (who supervises all national banks) had forced the board's hand. He had conveyed to key members of the board his concern over the rapidly falling profitability of the bank, its declining liquidity, and its inadequate capital. And he had broadly hinted that he would not be at all opposed to a proposal to merge Frontier with one of its younger, more dynamic, and better-managed competitors. Frontier speedily agreed that they had to look at the outside for a new chief executive officer. And they had little difficulty agreeing on a candidate. When they proposed Ross Abernathy's name to their colleagues, there was overwhelming approval. The comptroller of the currency—with whom such appointments are sometimes discussed in confidence—was clearly pleased: his comment was "I only hope you can get him." Abernathy was approached—and after a few weeks of negotiations he accepted, joined the bank as "president" two months before the old chairman officially retired, and then was elected chairman and chief executive officer.

Abernathy was then forty-seven. He had started out of high school in a medium-sized bank in Chicago, gotten his bachelor's and master's degrees at night at Northwestern while working for the bank, and risen rapidly. Together with another young officer—two years his senior—he had built his bank into a leadership position, first in Chicago, then in the country, then worldwide. And the design and development of the Chicago bank's international business had been entirely his doing, since the other young "comer"—he, like Abernathy an executive vice president—had, by agreement, devoted himself entirely to the domestic and especially the corporate business of the bank. Everybody at the Chicago bank knew that the next chief executive officer would be one of these two men. And the choice was indeed so narrow that the board split eight to seven. But the job went to Abernathy's slightly older colleague when the bank's former CEO retired in 1990—and that it was by only one vote did not make the pill any sweeter for the intensely ambitious and competitive Abernathy. He stayed on for one year as vice chairman. Then he left and moved to the city in which Frontier National Bank was located, as chairman and CEO of a group of insurance companies, established but stagnant companies. In three years he had turned them around—and in the process emerged as one of the leaders of the business community in his new hometown.

When the Frontier job was offered to him, Abernathy at first hesitated. He had worked terribly hard for three years, and he knew that Frontier would mean even more years of even harder work. He had met a good many Frontier executives and was not impressed by them. And he was not at all sure that Frontier could be turned around. The time to develop what Frontier lacked—especially the large corporate business, the pension-fund business, and the international business—seemed to him to have already passed. But then, Frontier had solid assets, especially a very good reputation and old and close ties with leading banks abroad. However, what persuaded Abernathy to take the job was that he realized that banking was in his blood. He missed the intellectual excitement of banking. He missed the stimulation of the international meetings—of the World Bank, of the International Monetary Fund, and so on—and the recognition he had been given at these meetings as one of the brightest younger bankers. And, as he had to admit to himself, the wound inflicted by being passed over in Chicago still rankled. So he took the job.

He was reasonably clear about what needed to be done. But he also knew that he needed a team to do it—and nothing he saw at Frontier made him feel that he had that team there. He could—and did—retire a large number of older executives. That was easy. Frontier, unlike most other large banks, did not retire senior people till they were seventy and, in some cases, continued them until seventy-two. So Abernathy simply had the board lower the retirement age for everybody to sixty-five. But the younger people serving under these old-timers did not seem to be any different. If anything, they were even more dispirited, even more convinced that "performance" meant taking care of whatever the office boy put into the in-basket and that banking was primarily a matter of belonging to the right country clubs. (Abernathy had never joined one and played tennis because, as he often said, "You can't discuss business over a volley.")

And so Abernathy did what he usually did when faced with a major personnel decision. He sought advice. There were three people to whom he usually turned; two were former professors of his, and the third was a lawyer and a member of the law firm that had led his former Chicago bank's legal business. He was not at all surprised when each of them gave him different advice—that was, after all, why he went to them. But he was surprised that he could not make up his mind which of the three to listen to—usually Abernathy had little difficulty deciding which advice to follow.

The first man said: "Look, Ross, you really have no choice. You can't fire forty people—you'd have no organization left. You have to develop the small team of top people you need out of the bank's human resources. You yourself say that the officers are technically competent. It's up to you to give them vision, to develop performance goals and performance standards, and to get them to where they make demands on themselves. Ask a very great deal of them. Make it clear that those who can't or won't live up to these demands will have to go. But also make it clear, first, that you are willing to support anyone who tries, and secondly, that achievement will be recognized and well rewarded. I don't see what else you can do—I know it means backbreaking work and a lot of disappointment. But there is no other choice, believe me."

The second professor said: "You have no choice, Ross, but to bring in a new top team—not a large one. Maybe only half a dozen people but people who know what performance means, and above all, people who know what you mean by performance, people you trust, people you understand, people who trust and understand you. That means people with whom you have worked closely in the past—in large part, of course, young enterprising people from your old Chicago bank. You don't have the time to develop the young MBAs you could hire from the business schools—you have to change the way the bank acts in a hurry. You have to make it clear to the entire bank that there has been a change. And anyone you bring in has to be able to make decisions and to give orders speaking for you, knowing what you are after, and in turn be trusted by you. There is no other choice, believe me."

The lawyer said: "Of course, you have to bring in a new team from the outside. You can't wait until the young hotshots from the B-schools are 'ready' fifteen years hence—by which time the old-timers in Frontier will have corrupted them anyhow. But, Ross, don't bring in your cronies. Bring in only people who have independently—and in banks with which YOU never had anything to do—proven their capacity to lead and to perform. For one, you will have to be completely objective about them. More important, the bank must feel that the new members of its top management team have been picked for proven performance capacity and not because they are your friends. It should not be hard to find such people. The major banks are full of people who are in the position in which you were in Chicago, that is, just an inch behind a front-runner a few years older but just as good as they are. You can offer them what their present bank cannot offer—a command position and a challenge. But stay away from Chicago. Any place but in Chicago or in the city you are in now. You don't want to raid your local competitors either. There is no other choice, believe me."

Confronted with these three mutually incompatible choices, each presented as inescapable, Abernathy sat down to analyze each alternative. He wrote out three headings: Inside Team, My Team, Outside Strangers. Then he wrote under each heading: (a) Pros, (b) Cons, (c) Risks, (d) Morale problems and morale advantages; and proceeded to list objectively the arguments for and against each proposed course of action—promising himself to keep opinion and judgment out of the exercise until completing it.

QUESTIONS

How would you fill out these analysis sheets? Please obey Abernathy's rule and refrain from any expression of preference, any argument, and any opinion until you have gone through the complete analysis. And indeed even then.

Case Number 31

The Failed Promotion

An old established and prosperous investment banking firm in New York City decided in the mid-1960s that it needed to strengthen its ability in international business. The firm did not want to go "multinational" itself. The senior partners were convinced that the kind of service they rendered was more akin to a professional practice than to a business, and they believed that a professional practice requires fairly small size and the close personal contact of the principals. Both the size and contact requirements were, they thought, incompatible with geographically dispersed operations. But they concluded that they needed in the senior management of the firm at least one person with extensive international experience and contacts. He would, they thought, build more or less permanent alliances with investment banks in Europe—perhaps even in Japan—which would enable the firm to acquire both the worldwide expertise and the worldwide banking network it needed to serve its clients.

No such person could be found within the bank. And so, for the first time in the fifty-year history of the firm, an outsider was brought in directly into a partnership. Frank McQuinn, aged thirty-five, had worked his way up in the international division of one of the big commercial banks. He had started and developed its Düsseldorf branch, moved on to head the large London branch and finally all European operations. McQuinn now wanted to return to the U.S. to live—his children were entering their teens. He knew that in his own bank he would not make it to the very top—he was at the wrong age for that, with a top-management team whose members were in their late forties only. He also knew that in his own bank he would have to move into domestic banking to make the next big step—and he loved international work. Also he saw a chance to build an estate in a private banking firm that, though legally incorporated, was, of course, actually a partnership.

So he joined the partnership—and worked out exceedingly well. Within two years he was promoted to senior partner and to membership in the five-man executive committee of the firm. The international business grew very fast and profitably. As a member of the executive committee McQuinn found himself drawn more and more into relationships with major clients in all areas, domestic as well as overseas. The international business grew so fast that he alone could not manage it. Accordingly, he discussed with his colleagues on the executive committee the desirability of bringing a second top man into his international department. With their consent in principle, he then picked Stanley Novack as deputy general manager—international, with a clear understanding that Novack would be made a partner if he worked out.

Novack was delighted. In his present position he had little hope of becoming a partner, for that very profitable honor was traditionally reserved for "bankers," that is, to people in charge of client relationships or operating functions. Novack, while highly respected in the bank, was an analyst—a very successful one who, at age thirty-one, had become chief of economic and securities analysis and the main adviser to the partners. He was also pleased because it was largely his analysis and recommendation that had pushed the firm into the international field and into bringing in McQuinn. From the first day, he had worked closely and well with McQuinn.

But it soon became clear that Novack was not working out as deputy head of International. What was wrong was not at all clear, but things just didn't get done. Decisions weren't made, deals were left hanging in midair. In short, McQuinn found that he had to do more himself than ever before. After eighteen months of this, Mc-

Quinn came to the conclusion that Novack had to go. And so he went to the chairman and chief executive director and said, "Novack isn't working out. He has turned out to be no good at all. I am afraid we have to let him go."

The chairman at first said nothing—for a very long time. Then he said gently, "You don't surprise me at all with the news that Novack isn't working out. Indeed I am only surprised that you waited so long before facing up to the disagreeable fact. I expected you in here nine months ago—and I hope you'll learn not to wait so long in the future before facing up to a disagreeable fact. Also," said the chairman, "I would have been greatly surprised if your decision about staffing International had worked out—regardless of whom you put in there. For you violated all the rules for making promotional decisions. And that's not hindsight. Here"—and the chairman pulled out the bottom drawer of his desk and whipped out a memorandum—"is what I wrote to my predecessor on the day you came in here and let me know that you had told Novack that YOU were going to put him in the job as your deputy."

McQuinn read the memo:

McQuinn has just been to see me to tell me that he has decided to appoint Stan Novack his deputy and has told this to
Novack. I am disturbed, for McQuinn clearly violated the rules
you so strongly emphasized for promotions. He settled on the
person rather than thinking through the requirements of the
job; he settled on one person rather than choosing three or
four candidates; and he settled on a man rather than discussing his choice(s) with a number of knowledgeable colleagues.
You taught us that a promotion decision made in violation of
these rules is almost bound to turn sour—and I have learned
the hard way that you are right. Shall I try to get McQuinn to
reconsider? I realize I have been remiss in not making sure that
McQuinn understands how we in the firm make major people
decisions. I am not willing to see Novack destroyed—he is

much too valuable a man. But I am reluctant also to overrule McQuinn in a decision within his area, especially one that he has already announced publicly. What is your advice?

And below the former chairman, who was now semiretired though still a partner, had written:

Keep this memo and wait—but be prepared to bail out both McQuinn and Novack!

"So you see, Frank," the chairman went on after McQuinn had read the memo, "I can't say I am surprised that Novack's promotion didn't take. But I am more than surprised, indeed I am shocked, at your attitude. The one thing we know for sure is that you made a mistake— for appointing Novack was your decision. To let Novack go, as you propose, because you made a mistake is not only grossly unfair and unjust. It is asinine. Why should we lose a man as valuable as Novack was all these years, and as achieving as he has been in every previous assignment, just because you made a mistake?"

McQuinn was taken aback. "I don't understand at all," he stammered. "Do you propose to leave Novack in a job he can't manage?"

"Of course not," said the chairman. "He is not doing the job and has to be relieved. We owe that to the firm, but we also owe that to him. But that's only the first and the easiest step. I expected you to come into my office first with a considered recommendation on what we should do with Novack now. Where does he belong in this firm? What can he do? What can he not do—and why? Has he, for instance, learned enough about operations through his eighteen months of failure and frustration that we should make him a partner in charge of analysis and research?—something we have never done, since we felt analysts didn't know enough to become partners. Should we move him into a totally different area? If so, which one? With whom should he work? Should he continue to work with you, or not? That's your responsibility—you put a performing man into the wrong position."

"And then," continued the chairman, "I expected you to come in and tell me why you think that Novack has not worked out. After all, he did well in every previous assignment he has had—and now he fails. That needs explanation, and you are the responsible man, the one who owes this explanation to the firm, to yourself, and, most of all, to Stan Novack."

McQuinn sat silently for several minutes. Clearly he was having difficulty taking in what he had heard. Then he said slowly, "I can see why you expect me to think through what we should be doing with Novack and why you reject my hasty conclusion that we have to let him go. And I am grateful to you for teaching me something I should have seen myself. But I am totally baffled by your second request. Isn't it clear what happened? Novack was promoted to a job that turned out to be beyond him, that's all."

"So you believe in the Peter Principle," said the chairman, with considerable sharpness. "Frank, believe me, that's nothing but an alibi for a lazy or incompetent executive—and I don't think you want to be either. There isn't the slightest reason to believe that a person who has performed well in a number of assignments will all of a sudden fail to perform in another assignment because he has reached his level of incompetence, whatever that may mean. On the contrary, it's far more likely that people who perform in a number of assignments will perform in the next one—performance is performance, after all.

"If they don't, there's got to be a reason. Once in a while the reason may be that they stop performing, stop working, get old, sick, or tired, burn out. But I don't think that's what happened to Stan Novack. It's far more likely that the reason was one of the three common reasons why promotions fail—all three primarily boss-failure rather than employee-failure. Either the promoted person keeps on doing what he or she did in the old assignment, oblivious of the fact that it's a new assignment and requires doing different things. And that happens always because the boss does not pull up the employee, does not require of him or her that he or she think through what the new job requires. Remember when you came here first, how we called you before the executive committee—three times at ninety-day intervals—and asked you to think through and let us know what your new job with us required of you? And every time you kind of asked us for guidance and we said, 'The only thing we are willing and able to tell you is that the new job requires different things from what the job you had at the commercial bank required.' Remember? Have you done this for Novack, or did you let him continue to do good analysis such as he had been doing for years? If so, don't blame Novack, blame yourself. You didn't do your part in making your promotional decision effective.

"Or have we learned that Novack is an analyst and temperamentally unable to hold a decision-making leadership position? Till you put him in as your deputy, he always acted as an analyst and adviser. Other people made the decisions. Maybe he just cannot take the burden of decisions. It's not uncommon. Even people as young as Novack can't always learn—it's a matter of personality as much as of knowledge or skill. And finally, perhaps the job you created and into which you put Novack, is an impossible job, a job no one can do. A job, for instance, in which a person must fail if he does what the boss used to do, but is also a failure if he does anything else. Or it may be a job in which he has to be both an assistant to and the actual head of the operation.

"You have two weeks," said the chairman, "to think through, first, what you recommend the firm should do with Stan Novack. We have to pull him out, and I shall do so today by asking him to take on an assignment for me, but in two weeks you have to make a recommendation. And it had better start out with the realization that a decision of yours has failed to pan out. And then, within two weeks, I also expect a reasoned and well-supported analysis of why Stan Novack didn't work out. Was it your failure to give him the guidance you should have given him? Was it wrong temperament? Then we will both know what kind of job Novack can take in the future and also what kind of person we need for the job you want to fill. Or do we have to redesign the job so that human beings can fill it? We have no right to ask people to take on jobs that will defeat them, no right to break good people. We don't have enough good young people to practice human sacrifice.

"Until you have thought through the reason why Novack's promotion failed, I shall not permit you to appoint anyone in Novack's place."

QUESTIONS

What do you think of the chairman's argument? What do you think of the rules for making a promotional decision that the former chairman had worked out? How can McQuinn go about answering the chairman's request and find out the reasons why Novack's promotion had failed?

Part VII

Managerial Skills

Case Number 32

Lyndon Johnson's Decision

When Lyndon Johnson was Senate majority leader during the Eisenhower years, he was adamantly opposed to any American involvement in Indochina. It was widely believed that it was his opposition that, in 1954 after the French defeat in Vietnam, made Eisenhower rule out any American military intervention—against the strong pressure for it on the part of his secretary of state, John Foster Dulles, his vice president, Richard Nixon, and his chairman of the joint chiefs of staff, Admiral Radford. Johnson continued his opposition to any American involvement in Indochina when he became President Kennedy's vice president. He was outspoken about his desire to withdraw the American advisers whom Eisenhower had sent to bolster the South Vietnamese regime; and he strongly opposed the plunge into Vietnamese politics on the part of the Kennedy administration when in the fall of 1963—shortly before President Kennedy's assassination—it countenanced the coup against President Ngo Dinh Diem and thereby made the American government the guarantor of the successor regime and the actual power in South Vietnam. Johnson continued this position after becoming president and resisted all through 1964 pressures for increased American involvement, especially from the foreign and defense secretaries he had inherited from Mr. Kennedy. He strongly emphasized during his election campaign of 1964 his resistance to any attempt to expand the war in Vietnam or to make it an American war. Indeed, his opposition to U.S. involvement in Vietnam was so great and so well known that it was widely feared in the Pentagon and the State Department—and even more in Saigon—that Johnson was encouraging the North Vietnamese to attack by, in effect, promising them that the U.S. would not resist.

Then, in the spring of 1965, Hanoi adopted a new and aggressive policy. Previously, Hanoi had confined itself to supporting insurgents in South Vietnam with arms, advisers, and money. It had, in other words, matched the American policy of support for the South Vietnamese government and also the American decision not to become involved militarily on a large scale. Beginning in the spring of 1965—only a few weeks after Johnson had been sworn in for his second term—North Vietnam began to send North Vietnamese regulars, heavily armed with Russian armor and artillery, into South Vietnam, where they took over military operations from the South Vietnamese Vietcong guerrillas. In late spring, these North Vietnamese troops—by now the equivalent of about fifteen American divisions—launched a massive attack clearly aimed at cutting South Vietnam into two. North Vietnam's objective suddenly seemed to be a "military solution," that is, the defeat and destruction of the South Vietnamese military.

In the face of this situation, Johnson changed his basic position. He decided that force had to be met with force. He sent a major American military force to Vietnam to take over the main burden of fighting the North Vietnamese. He argued—enough documents have been published to make this clear—that the South Vietnamese would not rise to join the North Vietnamese, as indeed they did not. In this situation, a defeat of Hanoi's military thrust would rapidly induce Hanoi to reestablish the uneasy truce that had prevailed before, if not to replace it, as had happened in Korea ten years earlier, with a long-term armistice. Militarily the United States was at first fully successful. The North Vietnamese were beaten back with very heavy losses in manpower and almost complete loss of their equipment. By fall of 1965, the North Vietnamese were in full retreat, pulling their badly mauled divisions back into North Vietnam. There was every reason to believe that Johnson's basic premise that such a defeat would lead to a valid armistice would be proven right. We know that active negotiations via Moscow were going on and that around Christmas, 1965, an armistice was thought "to be in the bag" in Moscow, apparently as well as in Washington.

What happened then we do not know. One theory is that Leonid Brezhnev, until then only one of the three top men in the Soviet hierarchy, made his bid for supreme power in late 1965 and needed the support of the military (and, it seems, especially of the navy), which he only got by turning "hawk." To support this theory there are the facts that Russia suddenly began to step up military supplies to Hanoi—after telling Hanoi and the world in 1965 that supplies would be limited to replacement of lost equipment; that, at the same time, the Soviet Union, after long hesitation, decided on a crash program to build a three-ocean navy; and that it took over supplying India with arms on a massive scale. Another theory argues that the balance of power in Hanoi, between "doves" and "hawks," shifted decisively toward the "hawks," as Ho Chi Minh suffered a heart attack or stroke and could no longer control events (though he did not die until 1969). Yet another theory—the least likely one, by the way—maintains that growing American resistance to the Vietnam War encouraged the Communists; but there was still very little resistance to the Vietnam War in this country in early 1966, though it was beginning to grow and to be more vocal.

In any event, by January or February, 1966, it had become clear that events were not following Lyndon Johnson's expectations. Hanoi had broken off truce negotiations. Instead it was pouring back supplies and men into South Vietnam. The Russians who, only a few months earlier, had acted as intermediaries between Washington and Hanoi were stepping up their support for Hanoi and refusing to use their influence to persuade Hanoi to moderate its demands for total surrender. And so President Johnson had to face the fact that his policy, despite its resounding military success, had been a political failure.

When he sat down with his advisers—mostly the crew he had inherited two years earlier from President Kennedy—no one felt very good about the situation. But the prevailing sentiment—and Johnson agreed reluctantly—was that there was really no choice but to hang on. It was now clear that the North Vietnamese could not win a military victory against American forces. It was equally clear that the South Vietnamese, while perhaps not enthusiastic about their regime, did not support the North Vietnamese government. So, the consensus ran, "sooner or later" Hanoi or their "real master," Moscow, would have to see the futility of the drive for a "military solution," and until then all the United States could do was to hang on.

No one liked this conclusion. But everyone—Dean Rusk, Robert McNamara, McGeorge Bundy, the Joint Chiefs of Staff—went along, reluctantly. The only dissenter in the group, according to all reports, was George Ball, undersecretary of state. He was primarily concerned with economic affairs and, until then, very far away from the Vietnam problem. Ball is reported to have said: "I don't know, Mr. President, what the right answer is. But I do know that continuing last year's policy is the wrong thing to do. It cannot work and must end in disaster. For it violates basic principles of decision making."

QUESTIONS

1. *What principles did George Ball have in mind?*
2. *Would you agree with what is said to have been Ball's point, that is, that there are "principles" of decision making and that to violate them dooms the decision?*

Case Number 33

The New Export Manager

Ever since it was founded in 1924, the Ridgewood Tool Company—a leading manufacturer of hand tools—had been in the export business. For many years an exporting firm in New York City had had the exclusive distribution of the company's products outside of the United States. Then, as exports grew, the company appointed distributors or agents in various foreign countries. An export manager was appointed in 1986; but he was mainly a clerk handling incoming orders from overseas and arranging for the collection, through the company's bank, of the monies due. By 1990, however, the company's export volume had grown to the point where this did not work anymore. And when the old export manager retired, management decided that the export business had to be properly managed and also had to be properly organized. Maybe, one of the directors mused, the company even had to set up its own facility in Germany, where the company's products were well known and popular. But there was no one in the company who knew anything about foreign business; and so a young, energetic fellow—Frank Andrews, aged thirty-five—was hired from International General Electric to become the new export manager. Andrews made a quick trip to visit the company's main foreign distributors and agents. Upon his return, he told the president of the company that he would work out a plan for the company's foreign business. And then he retired to his office. He appointed a veteran clerk in the export department as assistant export manager and gave him the job of handling the day-to-day business, which proceeded along at its accustomed donkey trot.

But *what did Andrews himself do*? He was at the office every day. People peeping through his office door—which he kept tightly closed most of the time—saw big stacks of books, papers, and reports, behind which Andrews's head was barely visible. BUT WHAT DID HE DO? After this had been going on for about four months, pressure on the president mounted to the point where he called Andrews into his office and said, "You have been here almost half a year—and none of us can figure out what you are doing." Andrews was clearly surprised. "Don't you see that I am studying?" he came back. "And until I can come in to you with a proper plan, what's the point in my wasting your time?" "Mr. Andrews," the president said, "you and we clearly made a mistake. I think it would be better if you looked for a job elsewhere."

The president, when he recounts this experience, confesses himself totally nonplussed. "The fellow came to us with a reputation as a dynamic take-charge, livewire," he says. "And clearly he must have something. Since leaving us, he has joined a very big company and is now their vice president for Europe and, I hear, doing very well. But he spent six months with us just sitting and doing nothing."

Andrews is not only nonplussed but still quite bitter. "These old fogies," he says, "just didn't realize that one has to plan an international business. They had no figures, no plans, no organization. They didn't hire me to peddle pliers but to get them into the world market the right way. What did they expect me to do except to work out the right plan?"

But one day when he said that to an old friend—an experienced lawyer with whom he had gone to college—he got an unexpected reply: "Sure, Frank," the friend said, "these people were 'old fogies.' But the fault was yours—you acted like a young, arrogant fool."

QUESTIONS

Can you explain to Andrews what his lawyer friend meant? And then, can you perhaps think through what the company and its president might have done to prevent what clearly was a total breakdown of communications?

Case Number 34

The Insane Junior High School Principal*

When the new city council of a well-known eastern suburb appointed a new school board in the mid-1960s, it gave it one mandate: Eliminate the extreme racial segregation in our public schools. In 1945, at the end of World War II, the town had been lily white; then the African-American influx began—mostly an African-American middle class fleeing the neighboring big city. By 1966, the town had an African-American population of 40 percent. But apart from the consolidated senior high school, whose 4,500 students contained an African-American minority of 30 percent, all schools in the town were strictly segregated—achieved mostly through dividing the school districts to fit segregated housing patterns. The worst cases were the five junior high schools. Four had big new buildings but their facilities were grossly underutilized; indeed they were half empty. And they were almost completely white. The fifth was a swollen monstrosity, running double shifts in an old, condemned, rickety building that had been slated to be torn down even before World War II; and it exceeded the state's fire and occupancy maxima by 50 to 60 percent in every room and on every shift. It was solidly African-American.

---

* This case was written for the sole purpose of illustrating the role of *perception* in effective communications. Although a tragic illustration, the case goes to the heart of what is required to achieve effective communications in race relations in particular and in human relations in general.

The new board set to work with a will. But it soon found itself up against serious resistance—almost sabotage—on the part of the African-American community. The very people who had screamed the loudest about racial segregation in the schools seemed unwilling to do anything—including the three highly respected African-American members of the seven-person board. Slowly and with great reluctance, the African-American board members hinted at the problem. Everybody knew, of course, that the fifth, the African-American junior high, would be closed and its students redistributed to the four newer, half-empty, and so far, white schools. Even then, these schools would be only moderately filled. Everybody knew that one junior high school principal would be kicked upstairs—probably into a job as assistant principal of the high school or assistant superintendent at the district level. All the white members assumed that Mr. Milgram, aged sixty-two and principal of one of the white schools, would be promoted, that is, be made to vacate the principalship. After all, he was within three years of retirement and altogether not the strongest principal in the system. But everybody in the African-American community knew something no one in the white community even suspected.

Mrs. Wicks, the African-American principal of the African-American junior high, was suffering from advanced mental illness. Where for years she had been "eccentric," her condition had worsened rapidly to the point where she was clearly psychotic half the time—a pretty advanced case of paranoia with violent episodes. Indeed, several years earlier, the African-American community, in an effort to protect her and others, had quietly taken steps to make sure that the poor woman would never be alone but would always be surrounded by a few sturdy, sensible, and reliable women members of the African-American community—this was after she had attacked one of her teachers with a pair of scissors and cut her around the wrist and the neck.

But, in 1966, Mrs. Wicks was the only African-American principal in the town. In fact, she was the only African-American principal in the state and, as such, a symbol of African-American achievement and a byword in every African-American home. Yet, should the school board have to reassign the principals, the principals would have to—according to state law—appear in person before the board, undergo questioning, develop their plan for the school they were applying for, and spend a grueling four to five hours with the school board. The sessions of the school board were public, well attended, and rather stormy, especially as the residents of one part of town—the part where Mr. Milgram's junior high was situated—were known to be strongly opposed to racial integration, were determined to fight it, and were certain to make things mighty unpleasant for any African-American candidate for the principalship of a "white" junior high. That Mrs. Wicks could get through such a session without losing her composure seemed most unlikely.

The problem "solved" itself. On a Sunday, during church service, the woman who had been detailed to watch poor Mrs. Wicks ceased to pay attention for a few minutes. Mrs. Wicks suddenly whipped out a kitchen knife, ran up to the altar, and attacked the African-American minister, stabbing him twice in the back. He survived, but, of course, she had to be hospitalized, and had to be removed from her job. However, the Saturday night before that, one of the African-American members of the school board—himself a respected physician in the community with a practice that antedated the postwar African-American influx and that was largely white middle-class—had taken the bull by the horns and had called a meeting of the board in his home.

"Look," he had said, "you people ought to know why we are dragging our feet—you ought to know about the problem with Mrs. Wicks. All of us on the board, African-American and white, have a communications problem. The African-American community does not really trust the board to keep all the African-American teachers at Mrs. Wicks's junior high when we close it—even though they know that we will need just as many teachers as before, if not more. But the idea that we will really, in the face of resistance from Mr. Milgram's district, move African-American teachers into white, or formerly white, schools and give them the same jobs and the same opportunities—that's hard for even me to believe and very hard for any other African-American. And that we are then going to appoint an African-American principal to one of these four schools—that no African-American community in this country can believe. And you know we'll face opposition from a good many whites who will at least urge us to wait until Milgram reaches retirement age in three years. Mrs. Wicks is a very, very sick woman—we in the African-American community all know this. But still, she made it when it wasn't easy—and all of us have for years looked at her with pride. What do you plan to do to communicate our commitment to integration—not only of students but of faculties and administrators?"

QUESTION

What would you answer?

Case Number 35

The Structure of a Business Decision

The Nakamura Lacquer Company of Kyoto, Japan, was one of the many hundred small handicraft shops making lacquerware for the daily table use of the Japanese people when the American GIs of the occupation army began to buy lacquerware as souvenirs. Young Mr. Nakamura, who in 1948 had just taken over the old family business, saw therein an opportunity, but soon found that traditional handicraft methods were both too slow and too expensive to supply this new demand. He developed ways of introducing simple methods of machine coating, machine polishing, and machine inspection into what had been purely a handicraft, carried out with the simplest tools. And while the American GI and his souvenir-hunting disappeared with the American occupation in 1952, Nakamura built a substantial business, employing several thousand men, and produced five hundred thousand sets of lacquer tableware each year for the Japanese mass-consumer market. The Nakamura "Chrysanthemum" brand has become Japan's best-known and best-selling brand—good quality, middle class, and dependable. Outside Japan, however, Nakamura did practically no business, except for occasionally selling to American tourists through his established Japanese outlets such as the big department stores.

This was the situation when early in 1980—with U.S. interest in things Japanese beginning to grow significantly—Mr. Nakamura received in rapid sequence two visitors from the United States, both very highly recommended and equipped with the very highest and best credentials.

"Mr. Nakamura," the first one said, "I am Phil Rose of the National China Company—VP marketing. As you probably know, we are the largest manufacturer of good-quality dinnerware in the United States with our 'Rose & Crown' brand, which accounts for almost 30 percent of total sales. We think that we can successfully introduce lacquer dinnerware to a small but discriminating public in the U.S. We have investigated the Japanese industry and found that you are by far the best and most modern producer. We are willing to give you a firm order for three years for annual purchases of four hundred thousand sets of your lacquer dinnerware at 5 percent more, delivered in Japan, than your Japanese jobbers pay you, provided the merchandise is made for us with our trademark 'Rose & Crown,' and provided that you undertake not to sell anyone else in the U.S. lacquerware either with your brand or with any other brand during that period."

Mr. Nakamura had scarcely recovered from this shock when the next visitor appeared. "I am Walter Semmelbach," he said, "Semmelbach, Semmelbach and Whittaker, Chicago—largest supplier of hotel and restaurant supplies in the States, and buyers of dinnerware and similar goods for a number of department stores. We think we can successfully introduce good-quality Japanese lacquer dinnerware to our market. In fact, all our customers are willing to try it out. We think there is a market for at least six hundred thousand sets a year. Within five years it should be a couple of million. We have investigated your industry and feel you are the only man in Japan who can exploit this opportunity. We don't ask you for a penny. We are willing to pay the full costs of introduction. We are willing to budget $1.5 million for the next two years for introduction and promotion. You don't owe us that money. All we ask of you is (a) that we get the exclusive representation for your "Chrysanthemum" brand for five years at standard commission rates, and (b) that the first 20 percent on all the sales we make during that time—which we figure is roughly

YOUR profit margin—be used to pay off the money we actually spend for promotion and introduction as certified by a firm of independent accountants we want you to name."

QUESTIONS

Assume that both men are bona fide and that both check out as first-rate connections to have. Mr. Nakamura, therefore, has to think the offers through seriously—but what is it he has to think through? What decision is he being asked to make? How, indeed, can one compare the two offers?

Case Number 36

The Corporate Control Panel

The new president and CEO of a large multinational chemical company had come up through the legal and financial areas. When he had joined the company, it had been small and regional, if not local. He first realized that its rapid growth required very different legal approaches from those his predecessor as house counsel had used; and his legal draftsmanship and legal advice were largely instrumental in enabling the company to grow into a big business. Then he had taken over as the company's chief financial officer, when the multinational expansion was well under way. Again he had realized that the existing financial structure and, even more, the existing financial information and control, had been outgrown; and again his leadership in developing far more sophisticated information systems had a lot to do with the smooth and rapid growth of the company and with its ability to integrate companies, especially European companies, smoothly into its structure after acquisition or merger.

But when the same man became chief executive officer, around 1990 or so, he was dismayed at the paper load that descended on him every working day. He believed firmly that a CEO has to be in close touch with people; he believed even more firmly that he had to have time to visit key people outside company headquarters, especially the key people in overseas affiliates, which, by 1996, accounted for almost 50 percent of the company's sales and profits and were growing faster than the U.S. business. And here he was chained to a desk and buried under figures and reports. That he himself, only a few years ago, had initiated most of these figures and reports and had been highly praised for doing so only added insult to the injury.

For a year he tried to do both, stay on top of the paper flood and manage the company—only to come to the conclusion that he was doing neither. He spent hours with the reports, to be sure; but he did not really understand what they were telling him and felt strongly that he was losing control. He also neglected the business and, above all, the people. When his most achieving research director quit and bluntly stated as his reason that he was not getting enough top-management time and attention, the CEO knew that he had to do something drastic.

Then he remembered Christine Tschudi—a young Swiss woman who had started in the French affiliate and had risen to controller there in a short time. She had then put in for a transfer to New York headquarters, as she wanted to get an advanced degree in information-and-control systems and had later written her PhD thesis on "The Corporate Control Panel" (the CEO had gotten a presentation copy and had laid it aside, since he didn't understand a word of it, or rather, there weren't many words in it; it was all equations, it seemed). She now served as assistant controller for the company's overseas affiliates and was rapidly making a name for herself. He called in Christine Tschudi and said, "I need a control panel, and I need it fast: It has to give us in top management all the information we need to have control of the company. It has to give us the information fast enough for us to take action—most of what I get is history by the time I get it. All of us in top management and top operating management have to get the same information and know what we are talking about. It has to highlight the areas where important things happen or do not happen so that we know what to focus on. And it has to be concise enough so that I can understand it by studying it one day a month and so that we can reach agreement on where action or study is required in a two-to-three-day session each month—a session which it will be your job to prepare. Don't rush," said the CEO. "I know I can't get it tomorrow, but I do expect a pilot model we can test and run out within three months, at the latest."

QUESTIONS

How would you go about designing such a "control panel"? Can it be done at all? Or is it something that sounds good and does not work in practice. What about the CEO's idea that it be the same for the whole senior management group, is it sound?

Part VIII

Innovation and Entrepreneurship

Case Number 37

Research Strategy and Business Objectives

Three pharmaceutical companies—Able, Baker, and Charlie—are among the most successful pharmaceutical businesses in the world. Able and Baker are very large. Charlie is medium-sized, but growing fast. All three companies spend about the same percentage of their revenues on research. There the similarity ends. Each of them approaches research quite differently.

Able—the oldest company and the leader in the industry since the end of World War I (also, the most global of the companies)—spends a great deal of research money on one carefully selected area at a time. It picks this area—an exceedingly risky decision—when pure research in the universities first indicates a genuine breakthrough. Then, long before commercial products exist, it hires the very best people in the field (usually those who have made the original breakthroughs in theory) and puts them to work. Its aim is to gain early leadership in a major area, acquire dominance in it, and then maintain this leadership position for years. Outside these areas, however, the company spends no research money and is perfectly willing not to be a factor at all. (The strategy arose in the 1920s, when the original work on vitamins was first published. The company hired the Nobel Prize–winning chemists who had done the work, brought in the biochemists and pharmacologists and medical people who developed vitamins, and became—within a few years—the world's largest supplier of vitamins.

Case Number 41

The Invincible
Life Assurance Company

The Invincible Life Assurance Company was, almost in the literal sense, the child of Philip Mulholland. He had founded the company shortly after World War I, when he was a young insurance salesman who had become convinced that a locally owned and locally managed company could give better service to the rapidly growing midwestern region than any of the established big life insurance companies in the East. He had built the company over the years, first into the leading life underwriter of its own territory, then into one of the leading companies in the nation. He had been a pioneer in developing new forms of insurance. Both group life insurance and employee pension plans were first sold and developed in the territory by the Invincible, for instance.

If the Invincible was Mulholland's child, it was also his life. During the first ten or twelve years of its existence, he literally lived in the office. Even weekends he spent mostly visiting salesmen, establishing new agencies, or personally settling claims. He had married in his twenties, but his wife's death after a few years of happy marriage left him lonely, a widower, and childless. And from then on to the end of his life, his whole existence turned around the Invincible. The last twenty years of his life he lived in a simple hotel suite three blocks away from the office, and he went to the hotel only to sleep.

Mulholland was a quiet man, held in respect and affection by everyone who knew him. When he died, it was no surprise to his friends to hear that he had given away most of his money to charity during his lifetime and that he had left his modest estate to establish scholarships for the education of his employees' children. Even though the company had long ago grown to a large size, he kept his small and unassuming office. He was particularly interested in helping younger people and used to spend long hours discussing their problems (and the challenge of life insurance) with whatever bright youngsters he would notice when walking through the office. In fact, American life insurance is sprinkled with Mulholland's "young men," people whom he had found, had trained, and had finally found positions for; and among them are some of the biggest names in American insurance today.

Yet, these very qualities resulted in total lack of order and organization in the company. Mulholland never boasted that he could do every job in an insurance company better than anyone else. Yet, everybody in the company was well aware that this was indeed the case. Also, the company had grown imperceptibly—and to Mr. Mulholland, it was still the small office in which he had started, alone with a rate table and a battered typewriter. As a result, all major—and most minor—decisions still automatically went up to him. He decided on salaries, for instance, for everybody, from office boys on up. There was officially an "underwriting committee" to pass on doubtful applications or on policies in excess of $100,000; the state insurance commissioners had insisted on such a committee. But the district sales managers usually "cleared" such policies with Mr. Mulholland on the telephone directly; and while Mulholland always intended to "bring it up" at the next committee meeting, he rarely did so. In fact, vacancies on the committee often went for years without being filled. New insurance policies and contracts—the "new products" of the life insurance business—Mr. Mulholland always worked out himself, using the actuarial department only to do the mechanical computations for him. And he personally looked over and decided every appointment or promotion. As a result, his executives were never allowed to do any but purely specialist work—and primarily routine work, operating along the lines determined by Mr. Mulholland himself.

Even worse were the results of his kindness and of his interest in young people. As the company prospered, Mr. Mulholland became very generous to the old-timers who had worked with him in the early days. Salaries in the company were a strict secret—only Mr. Mulholland knew what people were being paid. But it was an open secret that in every department there were old-timers whose salary was quite a bit higher than that of their superior. Also in every department there were bright young men who had come to Mr. Mulhoand's attention, who were being used by him—usually without telling the department head—for special assignments and who were often being paid for these assignments separately and in undisclosed amounts. Titles were used by Mr. Mulholland as a reward for special services rather than as indication of work and rank—with the result that there were about twenty-five vice presidents who reported to men who themselves did not have vice-presidential rank and title. And since Mr. Mulholland himself made all decisions, practically every man who carried any responsibility reported to him directly rather than to the department head. The exact number of men who were accountable only to the president—in name or in fact—had never been determined but was running close to a hundred.

As long as Mulholland lived, this worked fine. But Mr. Mulholland, the founder of the Invincible and the only president and chairman it had ever had, died suddenly a few weeks before his seventy-seventh birthday and the fiftieth anniversary of the founding of the company.

The board of directors met a few days later and unanimously, almost without discussion, elected James Wintress as the new president.

This was not much of a surprise to anyone in the company, except to Mr. Wintress himself. Wintress had, for fifteen years, been head of the Investment Department. He was not the oldest of the senior vice presidents, but the youngest. But since the others were all seventy or more, that made him the only possible candidate in the group. Also he was the only department head who had really managed; for Mr.

Mulholland had known that he himself lacked financial experience and left the investment decisions to this investment vice president. Wintress was also the one officer of the company who had any outside business experience; before joining the Invincible as a senior securities analyst, he had been a trust officer of an important bank. Finally, Wintress was the only vice president who was at all known to the board members, since Mulholland had left the presentation of investment recommendations for board decision to him.

Wintress himself was, however, quite surprised, and by no means only agreeably. He knew that none of the other senior men were young enough to be given the presidency. But at sixty-three, he considered himself far too old. Also he knew very little about any phase of life insurance except investment—Mulholland's way of operations had ensured that functions were quite isolated from one another— and in particular knew nothing about selling insurance, handling claims, and working out new policies. Indeed, Wintress had expected to retire in another two years, when, under the company's policy, he had the right to retire with three-quarters of his salary (there was no compulsory retirement age).

Wintress himself had been fully prepared to be asked by the board for his recommendation on how to fill the job. He had decided to urge that the new president be found on the outside among the many "Mulholland young men" who had made good after leaving the Invincible. In fact, he had several names in mind.

One reason for this recommendation—which he was never asked to make—was his awareness of the organizational chaos in the company. He figured that someone who had grown up in the Invincible and been trained by Mulholland would understand and appreciate the spirit of the place and the achievement of the old man, would respect and maintain both, and would not ruthlessly or carelessly hurt people and spirit in reorganizing the company. Yet, he thought, such a man, accustomed to better-organized companies, would know that the company needed radical reorganization. Finally, he figured that the men he had in mind—who were in their mid-forties or early fifties—

were young enough to carry through the big reorganization task that had to be faced.

What decided Wintress, after all, to accept the offer of the presidency, despite his age and relative inexperience, was precisely his concern with the reorganization of the company and with the difficult and painful decisions on people that had to be taken. He figured that the company could run along pretty nicely for five years on the technical and functional competence it had to a high degree. That he did not know too much about these functions would not matter too much, therefore. At the same time, he would have five years to put the organizational house in order and to leave a manageable company to his successor. And five years, he decided and made clear to the board, would be the maximum time span for which he would serve.

After having accepted, Wintress began to wonder, however, about how precisely he should go about the organization job. He felt he could not discuss his qualms with any of his directors, if only because that would have implied criticizing the dead Mulholland and, by implication, the board of directors, who had let him operate the way he did. He also felt strongly that he could not discuss the matter with any of his officers, as this was bound to get "on the grapevine" and to upset the entire company. He decided, therefore, to seek the advice of an old friend who had started out with him in the securities business forty years ago and who had, in the meantime, risen to become senior partner of an important investment banking firm. Mr. Amasa Gray was known to be a deep student of organization and had himself successfully reorganized many an industrial company. And he could be depended upon to be both discreet and disinterested.

After listening to Wintress for a couple of days, Gray summed up his advice in these words:

You know very well that you can't finish the organization job in five years. You will have to make far too many compromises with personalities, traditions, and decency for that. Also, no organization job is better than the understanding and support of the people in the organization—and you can't change habits and attitudes of the old-timers that fast. You also know that the time is short for the standard remedies, such as starting manager development of your young people—that's one of the things that won't bear fruit in less than ten or fifteen years, and you have at most five. Yet you know that you need real results—and need them fast. Not only are you going to need a successor in five years. Most of your executives are older than you are and will need to be replaced much sooner—yet you have no one to replace them with, and don't even know which people should be replaced, which jobs should be maintained, and what the qualifications for the candidates should be.

What you have to do is to work out a basic approach that clearly expresses the basic principles of organization, job structure, and staffing you believe to be right for the company. With these principles, no compromising can be allowed—you have to be ruthless in sticking to them if necessary. And you have to do enough actual reorganization, actual abolishing of jobs, actual straightening out of salaries, actual building of new functions and new organs, to make it clear to everyone in the company what you are after and that you mean business. First, you have to work out the approach. Then you have to decide what action measures you are going to take right away and why. After you have done this, you must discuss the plan with your board and with your top officers. And then you can—and probably should—also bring in outside help.

But until you have done this thinking job, you can only do harm by talking about it or by bringing in experts. And this thinking job only you can do. Give yourself three months to think through your approach and decide on basic principles—and forget until then all considerations of tradition, practicality, people, tactics, and so forth. I'll be very happy to sit down with you again after you have decided on the principles of your approach and plan; until then, even I could not help you very much.

Mr. Wintress was not exactly happy to hear this. He had hoped to be told how to do the job rather than what the job was. He was, however, honest enough to admit to himself that Gray was right— this was the president's job and one that could not be unloaded or delegated. Still, he had doubts. On the one hand he felt that Gray was not ambitious enough in his thinking, and that to have nothing but an approach within five years was not good enough. At the same time, he also felt that Gray was too demanding—"impersonal" he called it in his mind—with his requirement of "no compromising can be allowed—you have to be ruthless . . . if necessary." On the whole, however, he was impressed with Gray's argument. And so, after a few days of doubt, he sat down to figure out for himself what a right approach to the reorganization of the Invincible Life Assurance Company might be.

QUESTIONS

Where should Wintress start in his thinking? Are there any things Wintress could do that would surely be wrong and could not work? Are there any things Wintress could do that would surely be both right and relevant to his to his problems?

Case Number 42

The Failed Acquisition

Normally a successful acquisition is based on what the acquirer contributes to the acquisition and not on what the acquisition is expected to contribute to the acquirer. Generally an acquisition can become successful only if the acquirer has thought through in advance what his or her company can contribute to the company about to be acquired and has planned for it.

This contribution has to be something besides money. Money by itself is never enough. The contribution to the acquired business may be in technology. It may be in products. It may be in distribution. But it has to be something that gives the acquired business a new potential of performance. This contribution has to be thought through and planned for before the actual acquisition takes place. It has to become fact fairly fast.

Here are three actual examples. All seemed to be based on what the acquirer could supply the acquired firm. One of the large bank acquisitions of the last decade of the twentieth century was the acquisition of Citibank by Travelers, in 1998. Travelers paid $70 billion for Citibank shares.

And the acquisition was successful because the acquiring company, Travelers, had thought through and had planned what it could contribute to Citibank that would make a major difference.

Citibank is the world's only major commercial bank that has become truly transnational. It has established itself successfully in practically every country of the world and has, at the same time, built a transnational management. But in its products and services, Citibank was still primarily a traditional bank, and its distributive and management capacity way exceeded the products and services commercial banking can produce and deliver. And Travelers had a good many of these products and services.

What Travelers saw itself as being able to contribute was to greatly increase the volume of business the superb Citibank worldwide distribution system and management could sell, and at little or no extra cost.

The second example is Ito-Yokado, the Japanese retail giant. It had been built from scratch in less than fifty years, and its growth has almost entirely been by acquisition. And each acquisition was based on what the acquirer, Ito-Yokado, could contribute to the acquired business. Ito-Yokado systematically acquired the Japanese franchises of highly successful U.S. businesses.

But it acquired such franchises only after it had decided that it could make a major contribution, which would make the acquired franchise a bigger and better business in Japan than it already was in its native United States; and in most cases, Ito-Yokado actually made this happen.

The third example is the acquisition of Chrysler, the U.S. automobile company, by Daimler-Benz, a German company. And it was an *acquisition*, no matter how much the press releases at the time claimed that it was a "merger of equals."

Chrysler had the product, but it didn't have the markets. Its market was strictly the United States, which was no longer big enough for the tremendous design and production capacity that Chrysler possessed and which one apparently has to have to survive in an automobile market, which is a global market.

And Daimler-Benz thought they could bring to Chrysler their tremendous distribution capacity in the world's only growth markets for motorcars: Asia, especially South Asia, and Latin America.

In the most successful acquisitions, the contribution by the acquiring company actually transforms the acquired company. It changes it from what made it successful in the past into what will make it successful in the future. The acquired company becomes a different business altogether. That objective sounds fairly ambitious. How often does it actually happen in real business life?

Well, it happened in the first two examples. What about the third? The third acquisition did not produce the benefits expected by Daimler, and in 2007, Chrysler was sold to a large private equity firm in the United States.

QUESTIONS

What went wrong in the third example? Is the rule "The acquirer (Daimler) thinks through in advance what it can contribute to the acquired (Chrysler)" wrong, or is there another explanation for why this acquisition failed while the other two succeeded?

Case Number 43

Banco Mercantil: Organization Structure

Banco Mercantil is a banking giant of one of the major Latin-American countries. Its branches in the country's capital city are in almost every neighborhood. And the Banco Mercantil branch office on the main square is the most imposing building in most provincial towns and cities.

Until the late 1960s its hundreds of branches outside the capital city served primarily as providers of deposits to the capital. They had little lending business of their own. Ninety percent of the lending business was in the capital. In the capital, too, was practically all the corporate business, that is, the business with large companies. There, too, was all international business—mainly borrowing money abroad, in such major centers of international finance as New York, London, and Zurich, to lend to the bank's corporate customers—and invest-ment activities, including a rapidly growing business in managing pension funds of large domestic companies. Only the mortgage busi-ness—legally organized in a separate bank but operated as a division of Banco Mercantil—did substantial business in the provinces. Even that amounted to only some 20 percent of the total, because most population growth was in the capital.

As time went on things began to change dramatically. The capital city continued to grow, but since it was badly overcrowded, more and more of the growth occurred in what had formerly been sleepy provincial towns. The mortgage business felt this first. It grew much faster outside the capital than in the capital district. Then companies began to build factories in or near provincial cities to tap their labor supply and to be closer to markets. Finally, in the mid-1970s, commercial lending began to grow very rapidly in the major provincial cities as small businesses, trucking companies, shopping centers, and local government offices grew up to serve the expanding population in the provincial towns, many of which were rapidly becoming fair-sized cities.

The organization of Banco Mercantil reflected the country's traditional economic structure. There was a big capital-city division, headed by the bank's president and chief executive officer himself. Its hundreds of branches outside the capital reported through regional headquarters to the one executive vice president in charge of the "Zona Interior." He, in turn, reported to the president. Then there had been formed a corporate banking division, first within the capital-city division, then as a separate division. This, too, was headed by an executive vice president who also reported to the president. International banking, mortgage banking, and fiduciary banking (investment management, especially of pension funds) also had evolved into separate divisions, headquartered in the main office in the capital and headed by executive vice presidents reporting to the president. At first, this structure worked, but with the growth of provincial cities the Banco Mercantil had clearly outgrown its structure.

When a new president took over in 1984, he ordered a business plan—the first the bank had ever had. To hardly anyone's surprise, it showed that except for international banking most future growth of the bank would take place outside the capital city. Near the end of the twentieth century, the plan predicted, the share of the capital-city division in the bank's loans would be down to 30 percent (or less) from 65 percent in 1984. Corporate-division loans would grow to 30 percent of total loans, of which fully one third would be to large customers headquartered outside the capital. The Zona Interior branches would have 40 percent of the loans and well over 50 percent of the deposits. Most of the new business would be centered in seven large provincial cities, each already with a population of two million or more.

How should the bank be organized for this change in its markets? The new president appointed an organization task force with himself as chairman. After a year of study it came up with a plan for decentralization. It provided for the setting up of eight regional "banks." One of these, the largest, would be the Banco Mercantil in the capital city—in effect, the existing capital-city division. It would, as before, be headed by the bank's president. The other seven regional banks, each located in one of the provincial centers that had emerged as "key cities" in the country, would have full profit-and-loss responsibility and would be headed by a regional "president" who would also be an executive vice-president of the bank and who would be in full charge of all the branches in a region, in addition to being the head of the main office in his provincial capital. These seven, in turn, would report to a senior executive vice president in the capital city who would report to the bank's president. There would be vice presidents for corporate banking, fiduciary banking, international banking, and mortgage banking, each headquartered in the capital city and reporting to the president. There would be an executive vice president for bank operations—also in the capital city and reporting to the president. An executive committee of fourteen people—composed of the president, the senior executive vice president in charge of the regions, the executive VPs of corporate, fiduciary, international, and mortgage banking, the operations man, and the bank's lawyer—would be served by a small group of staff assistants: an economist, a business-development group, a planning group, and a personnel adviser.

When the plan was presented to the bank's senior executives, there was a storm of protest from the regions. They pointed out first that the plan violated the principles of genuine decentralization. The regional executive VPs were to have full business responsibility. Yet for rapidly growing parts of the business—corporate banking, fiduciary banking, and mortgage banking—they would have no direct responsibility. These activities were going to be done by headquarters divisions. The same applied to operations—that is, to the 70 percent of the bank's costs that are people. They further objected that their subordinate status was both wrong in terms of organization and contrary to the bank's strategy. "We expect the bank to grow the most in the regions outside of the capital city, yet the regions will still be treated as they were under the old 'Zona Interior' system and report to a capital-city executive VP rather than directly to the chief executive officer," the regional men pointed out. Finally, they strongly objected to perpetuating the tradition under which the president ran the capital-city division. "This means," they said, "that the president will have no time for us, will give us no attention, and will, inevitably, channel resources and good people to the capital city, when the growth opportunities and needs are outside."

The president had to concede that the critics had a case. He therefore asked them to come up with a counterproposal, which they did within a few weeks. Their plan provided for a president with no duties except being the bank's chief public spokesman and its chief liaison man with the country's government, with international financial institutions such as the World Bank, and with the labor unions. In addition, he would be available as a troubleshooter in dealing with the top managements of big corporate clients. But all operating work would be lodged in the heads of the regional banks—one for the capital city and one for each of the seven regions. They, with the head of the international division and under the chairmanship of the president, would constitute the executive committee. This would meet every week for at least a whole morning (and preferably not always in the capital city but at least twice a year in each of the major regions) and would make all decisions. International would remain an operating division. Corporate would become a hybrid—in part handling relations with large corporate customers itself, in part advising the regional banks on corporate business. Operations and mortgage banking would become staff departments and confined to planning policy, auditing, and training, with each region doing its own operating work and running its own mortgage business. Fiduciary, the regional men thought, should probably remain centralized for the time being. There wasn't enough fiduciary business in the regions, and anyhow, pension-fund customers (the main customers of the fiduciary division) would prefer to deal with one group of professional investment managers, economists, and actuaries.

The president was appalled at this proposal—it meant, as he pointed out, that he would have almost twenty men reporting to him, since there would still be, of course, a legal counsel, an economist, a business-development group, and a planning group, not to mention personnel and public relations. He felt strongly that decision-making authority would be totally diffused under this plan: even minor matters would become "political" and would be decided by politicking and logrolling in an executive council in which the president could always be outvoted. He was troubled by the proposed ambiguity of the role and function of corporate banking, fiduciary banking, and mortgage banking—part operating divisions, part staff advisers. He felt strongly that operations should be centralized. Above all, he felt that he would not have enough to do himself and would largely become a figurehead.

It took two years and the help of a large American consulting firm to hammer out a compromise. Instead of eight regions there are five—the capital city and four regions outside. Each is headed by an executive VP who reports to the president and is a member of the executive committee. The president no longer heads the capital-city division but is a full-time chief executive officer with full power to make final decisions. International, mortgage, and fiduciary banking are operating "banks"—in fact, each is called a "region," headed by an executive vice president who is a member of the executive committee and reports to the president. Corporate banking, headed by an executive VP reporting to the president and sitting on the executive committee, is a hybrid—80 percent a "bank" taking care of corporate clients directly; 20 percent an "adviser," planner, and policy maker; and above all, a trainer, for the corporate-banking business of the regional banks outside the capital city. The status of operations was left up in the air—its executive VP (also reporting to the president, also a member of the executive committee) is both "responsible to the president for setting up, initiating, and running efficient banking operations and for the training and supervision of operating personnel throughout the system" and for "advising and counseling the regional banks in carrying out their responsibility for efficient banking operations and for training and supervising operating personnel." All other functions—economics, planning, budgeting, business development, personnel, public relations, and a new marketing function that the consultants recommended—were put under a newly created senior VP of administration who attends meetings of the executive committee without being a member, and who reports to no one quite knows whom. The lawyer is, of course, still there too.

QUESTIONS

1. *How does each of these three alternative organization structures measure up to the criteria of decentralization? Which of them comes the closest to "federal decentralization"? Could it have worked? Which of them is "simulated decentralization"? And might any of them be perhaps not "decentralization" at all but a thinly disguised functional organization?*

2. *Decentralization means "decentralized operations with central control." The president's plan stressed "control," the regional heads' plan stressed "decentralized operations." The president's plan stressed the span of control—with only seven men reporting to the president. The regional heads' plan would have meant twenty men reporting to the president—clearly more than one man can supervise. But the second plan would have followed far more closely the logic of the business and the planned strategy, with its expectation of rapid growth in the regional centers. How does the plan that was finally worked out satisfy these conflicting requirements of "decentraliza-*

tion" and "central control," of the logic of organization and the dynamics of strategy?

3. How much sense does the new position of administrative VP make? Do the functions he heads belong together as building blocks of an organization? What can he actually do for the highly expert professionals who report to him? Would it be better to have these functions separate and working with the executive committee, as originally proposed?

Case Number 44

The Universal Electronics Company

Universal Electronics had for many years been active in Latin America. In fact, it had done better in Latin America than in the United States. While it never ranked higher than sixth or seventh in the U.S. electronics industry, it early became the leading manufacturer in most of the important Latin American markets. Subsidiaries in all Latin countries were managed by Universal's own managers but otherwise ran and operated as local companies, employing local personnel, and manufacturing and distributing their own local brand names. In 1970, the Latin American businesses accounted for about 20 percent of the company's income even though no more than 8 percent of the company's capital was invested in them. In cheap radios and radio tubes and in transmission and telephone equipment, the Latin-American businesses had shown much faster growth than had the U.S. parent company itself.

However, Universal had had no experience in international business except in Latin America until a chance dispute with an Italian licensee brought the company together with a young Italian lawyer, Dr. Federigo Manzoni. In 1970, Manzoni suggested that the best way to resolve the licensing dispute was to buy up the Italian licensee, a medium-sized company, badly in need of capital, but with a good name and excellent technical facilities. Out of this grew Universal's present European business—five major subsidiaries, all either wholly owned or majority-owned, all growing faster than the U.S. parent company, all more profitable, and all bought or expanded with very little money before the great growth period of the European Common market, Manzoni himself became president of the Italian company— the fastest-growing and most profitable of the lot. Largely through his energy, his vision of the European potential, and his great negotiating skills, Universal achieved the European growth that made it a proverbial "growth stock."

In 1974, Universal had gotten just enough license fees out of Europe to pay its European patent and license expenses. By 1987, 45 percent of Universal's income came from Europe. In Universal's ten-year plan that figure was expected to go up to 55 percent by 1995 with the absolute amount doubling within eight years.

The European business had been the "baby" of the company's president, Julian DeRoche. He had negotiated every major purchase in Europe himself. He had pushed the deals through his board of directors. He had worked, aided primarily by Manzoni, on revamping the acquired companies where necessary, on finding the first-rate people in them to whom to entrust the management, and—the most difficult job of all—on bringing together their technical and research people with those of the parent company. Beyond technical cooperation, which had become very close, and overall financial and top-management-personnel control, the individual companies were largely left to manage themselves under their own local management group, organized according to the customs and laws of each country.

Two of the Europeans, however—Dr. Manzoni and the president of the large German affiliate—were members of the Universal board in the United States.

As a result of the European acquisitions and of U.S. space contracts, Universal grew rapidly in personnel and sales during these years. What had been a $200 million company in 1970 sales brought in close to a billion dollars ten years later. Where there had been fewer than twenty thousand employees, there were, in 1987, well over one hundred thousand—spread over five continents (as the European affiliates themselves had branches, subsidiaries, or affiliates abroad).

Meanwhile DeRoche was not getting any younger. In 1986, anticipating his retirement and the need for a basic reorganization of the corporate structure, DeRoche had asked his senior staff vice president to design an organization structure that would be adequate to the needs of an international company. Traditionally, Universal had been a functionally organized manufacturing company—with vice presidents of research, engineering, manufacturing, marketing, finance, etc. There was, for instance, an executive vice president–defense production, whose job cut across all conceivable organization lines. Latin America was organized in an international division that both supervised manufacturing subsidiaries and export sales and spent most of its time, it seemed to outsiders, in mysterious foreign-exchange deals no one understood. At home, the Universal Electronics Distribution Company had been set up to sell and service Universal's consumer products. But despite all these amendments, Universal's fundamental organization concept was still the basic functional structure of a rather small-sized manufacturing company.

The staff vice president, a man thoroughly trained in organization planning in one of the big manufacturing companies before he had come to Universal in 1980, talked to a great many people in the company. He also made the circuit looking at the other major "international companies." Early in 1987, he came up with a blueprint that provided for four divisions: Defense and Space Electronics, Consumer Products, Industrial Products, and International. All activities of Universal outside the United States and Canada were to be lumped together in the International Division. On the president's staff and outside of this divisional structure, the plan provided for the typical "staff services"—from research to purchasing and personnel.

The staff vice president's own candidate for the job of division president–international was Dr. Manzoni, for whom he had great admiration. But in the course of a conversation about the progress of

European unification, Manzoni pointed out that it would still be difficult to put one European national over another. And to the direct question of whether an Italian could easily be the head of a company with German, French, Dutch, British, or other European affiliates, Manzoni had said bluntly that it could be done but that he would not envy the poor devil who'd have to do it. Reluctantly, the staff vice president therefore decided on another candidate: Axel Sorensen, Danish-born and a Danish-educated U.S. citizen, who had headed Universal do Brasil—the largest subsidiary before the expansion in Europe. Sorensen had advanced rapidly in the U.S. organization before going out to Colombia as chief engineer. From there he went to Brazil, first as local chief engineer, then as a successful and popular local president. However, to strengthen Sorensen—and also to save him travel—Manzoni was named deputy group president and chief of staff–Europe to the International Division.

When the staff vice president showed this draft to the president, DeRoche was impressed. This was roughly what he had hoped for. "Let's, for safety's sake, check with Manzoni first," he said. "He knows the Europeans better than we do, and we ought to talk to him before taking this up with our own top people."

Accordingly the staff vice president flew to Rome to show his outline to Manzoni. He was astounded when Manzoni—the quiet, polite, amiable Manzoni—exploded after one look at the chart. "This is both an insult and abject stupidity! I know you and like you, and I'd be willing to stay on trying to prevent your ruining your European operations if you go through with this. But I would only stay on as head of Italy. Nothing in the world would get me to take the 'deputy' job and thereby compound the insanity of this approach to the organization of an 'international company.' And believe me, if the German and the Frenchman running your two companies in these two countries ever get wind of this harebrained scheme, they will quit within the week. They don't have to work for Universal. There are plenty of jobs for first-rate people in Europe today. And they won't be treated as if they ran an army and navy surplus store in Tibet instead of a large electronics company in their own country and one that contributes as much to total earnings as any of Universal's U.S. businesses."

The outburst was so violent that the staff VP thought it better to not even try to find out what Manzoni objected to—though the VP was completely bewildered.

QUESTIONS

What might it be that struck Manzoni as wrong? In what way does the staff vice president's approach, which does not differ much from the way in which a great many U.S companies organize their "international" business, differ from what you or Manzoni would consider the proper organization for a truly "international business"? (One clue: Is it in line with the economic realities and expectations of the company?)

Case Number 45

Research Coordination in the Pharmaceutical Industry

One of the country's, and the world's, largest pharmaceutical companies has major research laboratories in five countries: the United States, Great Britain, Ireland, France, and Japan. The laboratory in the United States goes back to the 1920s. The one in Great Britain grew out of work in World War II, when the company was among the pioneers in large-scale production of penicillin. The fundamental knowledge about antibiotics was then still primarily in Great Britain, so the necessary massive scientific and technical effort had to be based there. The Irish laboratory was a by-product of the decision to take advantage of exceedingly favorable Irish tax laws when locating a major new plant—a plant meant to produce intermediates primarily for the European market. Since the techniques used in the plant were mostly new, there was a need for a substantial group of technical and scientific plant-chemists, as well as plant-engineers. This made it logical for the Irish government to suggest that the company build a full-scale research lab, if only to hold well-trained Irish scientists in Ireland rather than have them emigrate to the United Kingdom, the United States, and Canada, and logical that the company pick up the suggestion. France was chosen for a laboratory in veterinary products, an old French specialty and one in which the French government and

French universities gladly cooperate with industry. Also, the French scientists the company wanted for the work were rather cool to the idea of moving to the United States and positively icy about the alternative suggestion: to move to the British midlands and to exchange the climate and scenery of the Loire for the fogs of Manchester. Japan first came with a joint venture. But when the American company bought out the Japanese partner in 1988, as the Japanese business grew so fast and so successfully that the Japanese could no longer finance it, it had to take over a large, flourishing, and completely Japanese lab. At first, only one man understood enough English to participate intelligently in the company's annual worldwide research conference. But that did not stop the Japanese from doing first-rate work in tropical medicine, in which none of the company's other labs had much competence or strength.

However, ALL five labs complained that there wasn't any coordination among them—there was constant duplication of effort; worse still, important and promising work wasn't being done at all because each lab thought another one was doing it; and no one in any of the five labs really knew where to go in the other four to find help, to get advice, and to talk over matters of common interest.

This was the situation when a new company-wide research vice president took over. Or rather, Dr. Rodney VanDelden—Dutch-born, American-educated, chief biochemist in the British lab until he moved to America around 1988 to finish a research job on central-nervous-system drugs the American group had botched—was really the FIRST company-wide research chief ever. His predecessor had still been research director in the United States, the first among five equals, and expected only to "coordinate." VanDelden was expected to MANAGE and had, as a visible sign of his new authority, control of the budgets of all the research labs, whereas formerly each country had set and managed the research budget for its own research efforts.

QUESTIONS

What alternatives does VanDelden have? What problems can he anticipate? What patterns of coordination and organization are available to him? And how could he test each of them to see which might be applicable in this multinational, multilingual, multidisciplinary, and multicultural setting?

Case Number 46

The Aftermath of Tyranny

The Rasumofsky Company, makers of "59" brand insecticides and industrial chemicals, had been run for many years by one man, Ferdinand Bullock, who was largely responsible for its steady growth during the previous seventeen years. Bullock had actually been the boss in all but title even before he had been made executive vice president in 1979. Since then, however, he had controlled everything in the company and made every important decision.

The president had confined himself to handling a few old customers—who half a century earlier had accounted for the bulk of the company's sales and whose loyalty and, on one occasion, financial help had pulled the company through the Great Depression. By now, however, these customers accounted for only 10 percent or less of the company's business—a result of the expansion since Bullock had become the dominant force in the company. The president, in other words, was not much more than an assistant sales manager except in title.

The other officers of the company were all Bullock's office boys and were treated by him as such. The only one showing signs of independence was Stanley Greenback, the assistant controller, who had come in from the company's public accounting firm four years earlier to handle tax matters; but he was still very young and had had no experience except in auditing and taxes.

The chairman of the board—the last representative of the Rasumofsky family that had started the company and had originally owned it entirely—had been worrying about the situation for quite some time. But he consoled himself with the thought that there was plenty of time, after all. Bullock was a young man, barely fifty-five, and had at least another ten years to go. And there was no doubt that the company prospered under his reign. Also, secretly, the chairman had little stomach for a fight with Bullock and was even afraid that in such a fight the other major stockholders, including various Rasumofsky widows, nieces, and granddaughters, would side with Bullock against him. The bulk of the shares, by the way, were owned by small shareholders outside. The shares had been fairly widely distributed when the company became publicly owned in 1928; and Bullock controlled the proxy machine.

Then suddenly, in early 1993, Bullock died of a heart attack. On paper that should have made little difference; in fact the organization chart looked prettier without him and with the functional VPs reporting directly to the president. But actually the company was without a head.

At the same time, Bullock's death released an emotional storm that had long been suppressed by his heavy hand. It became clear, even to the not-too-observant president and chairman, that Bullock had governed through fear and intimidation, that he had systematically driven out or broken people of independence and spirit and had replaced them with yes-people, and that even his own creatures in the vice presidential seats would not accept another "one-person regime." But, alas, it became also clear that not one of the VPs was able to stand on his own feet and to make his own decisions; they had all been too dependent on the strongman for too long.

QUESTIONS

What do you think the company can do? Can you make any general conclusions and observations on management theory and management practice?

Case Number 47

What Is the Contribution of Bigness?

Founded in the 1890s, the Miller Tool Company had been growing unspectacularly for ninety years when a new president took over around 1980. During the Depression, the company had almost been forced into receivership. But during and since World War II, it had become a leader in the design and manufacturing of metalworking machinery. The new president, McFettridge, however, felt, strongly that the prosperity of the company would not continue unless it did two things. First, branch out from traditional mechanical machine tools into the new electronic tools that McFettridge saw evolving in the field of automation. However, the company had no expertise in the field of electronics at all. Second, McFettridge argued, the company had to counter-balance its exclusive dependence on the heavy industries by a having stake in industries that were less vulnerable to economic fluctuations.

The company had sometime during the 1920s obtained a listing on the New York Stock Exchange. Hence, McFettridge could offer to the owners of small companies an exchange of their unlisted shares against Miller Tool's listed shares, with their tax advantages and greater liquidity. Armed with this, the considerable cash in the company's treasury, and its reputation, McFettridge stepped out to systematically acquire new businesses.

First, McFettridge acquired five electronics companies, all small and all highly specialized. To "diversify" the company's economic risk, he then added six companies in various service businesses, among them a trucking company, a building-maintenance business, a construction company (specializing in schools, highways, and other public works), a small chain of dry cleaning stores, and so on. He also bought seven small businesses that could not be easily classified, businesses that appeared to him to be sound growth investments and available at a reasonable price. The largest of them was a baking company with a good position in the Southeast, which McFettridge considered a growth region.

McFettridge died suddenly in 1989, at the time when the company he had built had acquired a reputation as an aggressive growth company and had become a favorite investment for some of the more adventurous of the investment and pension funds. Since he had still been quite a young man, nobody had considered the question of who could replace him; and there was no one in the company suitable to take over.

The directors brought in an experienced executive, Henry Augener, who, a few years before, had left the vice presidency of one of the big appliance companies to become a partner in a management-consulting firm. Augener, who came in as president, brought along with him Eugene De Witt, a younger man with a sound financial background.

The two men spent several months examining the company. What they found appalled them. Augener had been warned by some of his friends before he took the job that there was trouble ahead and that things were by no means as rosy as they looked in the write-ups of the financial analysts. But reality was much worse than anything anybody on the outside expected.

In the first place, none of the acquisitions really had much of a business. The old Miller Tool Company, with its $70 million of sales, contributed about a quarter of the company's sales and a considerably larger share of the company's profits. The largest of the additional businesses had only about $15 million in sales (the baking company); and the smallest had barely $2 million. Miller Tool, in other words, consisted of a large number of small businesses.

At the same time, these businesses had not been integrated with one another but remained completely separate—and it was hard to see how they could be integrated. None of the electronics businesses had contributed anything to the machine tool business. On the contrary, each of them was developing along its own lines. One of them was exclusively engaged in research work for the armed forces. Another one made component parts for the television industry in which it had to compete against very large and efficient manufacturers turning out the same component parts by the millions. The technological changes that McFettridge had anticipated eight years earlier with respect to the machine tool business were slowly coming in; but Miller still had many of the same tools it had had in the years following World War II. And it was clear that any change in the business cycle would result in a sharp deterioration for Miller with its obsolescent product line. At the same time, many of the good people at Miller had been sucked into new businesses that were in dire need of first-rate engineers and designers, so that Miller's design staff had become denuded of men and of ideas.

Things were in a similar state in the service businesses.

Even after six months of hard study, Augener and De Witt still did not quite really know what the company had in all its miscellaneous businesses, or where those businesses were headed. But while it was very clear that things were not in good shape, it was very difficult to say what could or should be done.

It was, for instance, quite clear that the company should get out of some of its businesses. But which ones should be divested? The ones with the least growth potential were also the businesses that contributed the most cash to the parent company—and cash was badly needed. At the same time, the companies with the best long-range potential for growth and profit were also those that needed the most cash, that indeed needed much more cash than the company could generate or obtain and that were also particularly risky or made high demands on technological leadership.

But the most pressing area was that of top management. It was clear to Augener and De Witt that the company needed a top management. McFettridge had run the show himself. He had brought in a large number of "bright young boys" whom he used as his messengers. But he himself, huddling with his "bright young boys," had made all the decisions. Augener and De Witt realized that there had to be a management at the top.

Equally important, there had to be management of the businesses. McFettridge had been able to get a number of businesses at very reasonable terms because he offered a way out to elderly owner-managers who had reached retirement age. These men themselves had usually run a very thin management, and when they pulled out, there was no one there. Then McFettridge had "replaced" them by taking over the management of the different businesses himself.

Augener and De Witt realized clearly that there had to be a management responsible for the performance of a business. But first, what was a business in their situation? Second, where would a management come from? Good professional managers, they realized, would hardly be interested in taking over such very small businesses. Entrepreneurs on the other hand, would much prefer to build their own business and to develop an ownership stake.

But the central question to which they returned again and again was that of corporate top management, its function, its structure, and its responsibility.

The two men spent several more months in fruitless discussions and analysis without being able to reach any decision on where and how to begin the difficult job. One day De Witt said, "Look here, we are never going to get anywhere trying to talk about any one of the individual businesses. We have to find a general approach. And we have to start out from the few things we can take as proven, we can assume are so.

"We know that this is a company with $300 million or so in sales that engaged in a lot of highly technical businesses in very competitive fields. We know, therefore, that it has to have the type of management of a big company, with its formal structure, with its highly paid specialists, and so on. We know that this management must contribute something to justify its very high cost. This much we know—everything else we are merely guessing at. So let's start out with the fact that this is a big company that requires a big-company management. What is the contribution that bigness and the management appropriate to it makes to a business? What is the justification for the expense? And which of our businesses are actually or potentially businesses that can justify, if not demand, big-business management? It seems to me that this is our first question. Those businesses that are not and will not be the kind of businesses suitable for big-business management are definitely not for us. We ought to get rid of them, regardless of the cash they produce or the growth opportunities they have, if only because they will never realize those growth opportunities under this big-company management. The others we will have to find a way to manage."

Augener thought a while and then answered: "You know, Gene, this sounds usable, but there are two things that bother me, two things I don't think I understand. First, I'm not quite convinced that there are lines of business that are 'small-business' or 'big-business.' I always thought that you develop the management that fits the size you deal with—and here you talk about businesses that are suitable for small-business management or for big-business management.

"And second, I am bothered by an implication in your approach: that a management should be able to manage, regardless of the industry or the line of business, only if certain management approaches and management methods, namely those applicable to big business, are valid. Is there no limit to the number of businesses or their diversity that one management can organize and manage?"

QUESTIONS

What do you think of these two questions? And how would you answer them?

Part X

New Demands on the Individual

Case Number 48

The Function of the Chief Executive

Although the mandatory retirement age at this company was sixty-five, John Neyland, the president, decided to retire at sixty-two. He was sixty when he made this decision. He had come in as chief executive officer of the company twenty-one years earlier. During his tenure the company had grown and prospered. He enjoyed his work, but lately he had noticed a tendency to tire more rapidly than in the past. Also Neyland, a devoted churchman, felt that he could contribute a good deal to his church, and especially to the colleges affiliated with it. For the last five years, he had served on the board of advisers for higher education of his church. He had greatly enjoyed the work and had felt that he was not really doing as much as was needed—especially at a time like the present, when the colleges were faced with tremendous demands for money, facilities, and faculty, let alone serious questions regarding their educational policy.

But what convinced John Neyland to step out earlier than he had to was the fact that he felt sure of having a first-rate successor. When Neyland had joined the company, Bill Strong was a very young accountant, fresh out of college. He was, however, already considered a very able man. When Neyland needed a young analyst to help him with a difficult tax negotiation during the Savings and Loan Crisis, Strong had been put on his staff. Shortly thereafter Strong became assistant to the president and, three years ago, vice president in charge of administration. Neyland felt certain that Strong could easily step into his job, felt, indeed, that Strong was likely to do a better job than he himself had done.

Before Neyland announced his intention to the board, he thought it best to discuss it with his closest and oldest friend on the board, the man who, many years earlier, had brought him to the company and who represented the largest and most influential group of shareholders. This friend agreed with Neyland's decision to retire early. But he disagreed violently with Neyland's nomination of Strong as his successor. "You know," he said, "that I have never voted against management, and that it is against my principles to do so. But if you propose Strong as your successor, I will vote against him and will make an issue of it. There is a capable successor in the company, but it is not Strong. It is Margaret Wetherall, your vice president of manufacturing. Strong has never in his life done any operating work. He has been a staff man all along. His only experience is in finance. Wetherall, on the other hand, started out as a design engineer, has been a sales manager, and has now run manufacturing for ten years. She really knows the business. And also, Strong has never had an independent responsibility. He has always been an assistant to you rather than responsible for results himself."

Neyland protested. "But look at the jobs Strong has done. You yourself have considered them outstanding. Strong did most of the thinking behind the basic change in our direction fifteen years ago to which we owe our growth. He does all the thinking behind our financing. And he has really been the one who has developed people and made the decisions about whom to put where. It was his courage that shifted Margaret Wetherall out of the sales job into manufacturing management. He is by far the best thinker we have. And you yourself have stressed often enough that he is a man of courage and integrity. Wetherall is a perfectly fine operating manager. But she has neither the imagination nor the ability to think that is needed for the top job."

"I don't think, John," his friend answered, "we will get anywhere on this by discussing people. You have made up your mind for Strong;

I have made up my mind against him. But we ought not to talk people. We ought to talk about the function of the chief executive and the job to be done. I think on that we disagree. I think we agree on the qualities of the individuals. Why don't you go back and think through what, in your mind, the chief executive of this company has to do, what he is responsible for, what his function is and what his qualification ought to be. I'll do the same. I'm sure we won't agree—otherwise, we would have agreed on the candidate. But at least after we have done this, we will be able to find out why we disagree. And I think you and I better agree before we bring this up with our colleagues on the board."

QUESTIONS

What do you think is John Neyland's concept of the functions of the chief executive? How does his friend see the job? By the way, do you think the friend is right in starting out with an objective idea of the function? Or do you think it would be better to begin with an outstanding candidate—or candidates—and then adapt the job to who he or she is and how he or she does the work?

Case Number 49

Drucker's Ideas for School Reform*

For sixty-five years, from 1939 to 2005, Peter Drucker published books and articles on various aspects of business and organizational leadership. But Drucker has also written about the problems of education and how they might be solved. Concerning education, here are three initial overall questions we had about his work: The questions are

1. Does Peter Drucker have the best ideas for how to go about reforming all of U.S. education, not just the teaching of a handful of teachers?

2. Are his best ideas included in the discussion below, or have we missed any?

3. Or if Drucker does not have the best ideas to go about reforming education, who does?

---

* This case has been adapted by permission from a working paper prepared by Kenneth G. Wilson and Constance K. Barsky, "Learning by Redesign," the Ohio State University, October 10, 2006. Kenneth G. Wilson received the Nobel Prize in Physics in 1982.

OUR PERCEPTION OF DRUCKER'S BEST IDEAS

Drucker's 1985 book *Innovation and Entrepreneurship** includes a number of brief references to education as an opportunity for new and appropriately planned entrepreneurial ventures. For one example, Drucker writes, "Perhaps the time has come for an entrepreneur to start schools based on what we know about learning, rather than on the old wives' tales about it that have been handed down through the ages." (110) He also offers a considerable variety of "sources" for innovation in chapters 3 through 9 and a number of alternative "entrepreneurial strategies" to choose from as well in chapters 16 through 19. Chapters 36 and 37 of his *Management, Revised Edition* (2008) summarize these sources of innovation and entrepreneurial strategies.

IE includes everything from some major concepts applicable to the whole subject of reform to a large number of "one-liners" that Drucker throws out but does not pursue further. We will review our nominees for Drucker's best ideas for education as found in *IE*, use these as a background to raise five further questions about education for discussion, and provide tentative answers of our own that need to be critiqued and evaluated. Then we will return to the three questions posed at the outset.

DRUCKER'S FIRST IDEA—RESOURCES

One concept in *IE* is Drucker's definition of "resources." He explains, "[Innovation] is the act that endows resources with a new capacity to create wealth. Innovation, indeed, creates a resource. There is no such thing as a 'resource' until man finds a use for something in nature and thus endows it with economic value. Until then, every plant is a weed and every mineral just another rock. Not much more than a century ago, neither mineral oil seeping out of the ground nor bauxite, the ore of aluminum, were resources." (30) He goes on to say, "The same holds just as true in the social and economic spheres. There is no greater resource in an economy than 'purchasing power.' But purchasing power

---

* Drucker, Peter, 1985, *Innovation and Entrepreneurship*, New York: Harper & Row. All numbers in parentheses following quotations are pages from *IE*, unless otherwise footnoted.

is the creation of the innovating entrepreneur." (30) Later, he points out, "What really made universal schooling possible—more so than the popular commitment to the value of education, the systematic training of teachers in schools of education, or pedagogic theory—was that lowly innovation, the textbook." (31) He claims that the textbook enabled teachers to successfully teach far more students than was possible without it. Our first question is about resources for education.

1. What resources are already available in education and are just waiting to be endowed with a "capacity to create wealth"?

Our answer, in brief, is that the students, who constitute 80 percent or more of all the people in a school, are the most promising underutilized resource.*

DRUCKER'S SECOND IDEA—CHANGES AS A SECOND SOURCE OF INNOVATIONS

The other major concept we highlight is Drucker's notion of "changes" that are sources for innovative opportunities. He writes (in his italics): *"Systematic innovation therefore consists in the purposeful and organized search for changes, and in the systematic analysis of the opportunities such changes might offer for economic or social innovation."* (35)

He makes his concept of "changes" more concrete throughout chapters 3 through 9, which review a long list of different kinds of societal changes that can be "sources for economic or social innovation." Our second question about changes relevant to education reform is, in brief:

2. What are the changes occurring right now that provide the most promising sources for major innovations in education?

One key change now occurring is that enough knowledge from enough distinct areas of research relevant to education has accumulated—one

---

* For two distinct perspectives on what students can do, see Cary Cherniss, 2006, *School Change and the MicroSociety Program*, Thousand Oaks, CA: Corwin Press, and especially, Louis V. Gerstner, Jr., et al, 1994, *Reinventing Education: Entrepreneurship in America's Public Schools*, New York: Dutton Group, pp. 244–245.

being learning theory from psychology (as mentioned by Drucker). It is now possible to identify and produce the missing knowledges needed for a knowledge-based innovation in education. Moreover, there are enough unexpected successes and other kinds of changes occurring to make an innovation somewhat less risky than it would be if it were based only on new knowledge. It took us ten years to learn enough about all these areas of research to be able to recognize what knowledges are still needed, as of *today*, and to develop the bare and preliminary outlines of a plan for producing them and launching innovations (far more than one) based on this combined knowledge.*

In *IE* Drucker wrote on his success as an innovator based upon the combination of existing and produced knowledge:

> My own success as an innovator in the management field was based on a similar analysis in the early 1940s. Many of the required pieces of knowledge were already available: organization theory, for instance, but also quite a bit of knowledge about managing work and worker. My analysis showed, however, that these pieces were scattered and lodged in a half a dozen different disciplines. Then I found which key knowledges were missing: purpose of a business; any knowledge of the work and structure of top management; what we now term "business policy" and "strategy"; objectives; and so on. All of the missing knowledges, I decided, could be produced. But without such analysis, I could never have known what they were or what they were missing. (116)

The next set of questions is based on three of Drucker's more specific ideas. The questions will follow a review of these ideas.

---

* We cannot discuss all the knowledges that we explore in this short case, let alone a plan for making use of these knowledges. But we note the crucial role that evaluation *based solidly on education research* played in the evaluation and the ongoing evolution of the New American Schools initiative, established in 1991 by leaders of the business community at the behest of former President George H. W. Bush. See, e.g., Mark Berends, Susan J. Bodilly, and Sheila Nataraj Kirby, 2002, *Facing the Challenges of Whole School Reform: New American Schools After a Decade*, Santa Monica, CA: Rand Corporation.

DRUCKER'S THIRD IDEA—UNEXPECTED SUCCESS

Drucker makes clear that there are sources of innovation that should be *relatively easy* to pursue, as opposed to one source of innovation that is *very daunting* to pursue. For example, the first relatively easy source of innovation that he discussed is the "unexpected success." (37–46)

No other area offers richer opportunities for successful innovation than the unexpected success. In no other area are innovative opportunities less risky and their pursuit less arduous. Yet the unexpected success is almost totally neglected; worse, managements tend to actively reject it. (37)

Drucker goes on to provide examples of managements that rejected an unexpected success in their own businesses, and of other managements that gained very substantial markets because they took advantage of their unexpected successes. But he also makes clear that taking advantage of an unexpected success involves a lot of hard work.

Managements must look at every unexpected success with the questions:

1. What would it mean to us if we exploited it?

2. Where could it lead us?

3. What would we have to do to convert it into an opportunity? And

4. How do we go about it? (45)

Moreover, Drucker writes, "The unexpected success is an opportunity, but it makes demands. It demands to be taken seriously. It demands to be staffed with the *ablest people available* [italics added], rather than with whomever we can spare. It demands seriousness and support on the part of management equal to the size of the opportunity. And the opportunity can be considerable." (45–46) This description of what management actually has to do does not sound *easy* or *simple* to us. Moreover, in the case of education, we found it is not very hard to identify examples of unexpected successes; they can be as obvious as a highly exceptional teacher who is accomplishing wonders with her students. But the problem we struggled with (to oversimplify greatly) is that a single highly exceptional teacher cannot substitute for the entirety of the 3 million teachers that the United States currently relies on for the education of its 40 million students.

DRUCKER'S FOURTH IDEA—
NEW KNOWLEDGE AS A SOURCE OF INNOVATION

Drucker also discusses a source for an innovation that he characterizes as extremely difficult to deal with, namely, new knowledge, discussed in chapter 9 of his book. It is "temperamental, capricious, and hard to manage" (107), and to make matters far worse, at least in the case of education, "knowledge-based innovation has the longest lead time of all innovations.

1. There is, first, a long time span between the emergence of new knowledge and its becoming applicable to technology.

2. And then there is a long time period before the new technology turns into products, processes, or services in the marketplace. (107)

   [He later says:] The lead time for knowledge to become applicable technology and begin to be accepted in the marketplace is between twenty-five and thirty-five years. (110)

Yet, when it comes to education, Drucker indicates that it may be time to pursue new knowledge as a source for innovations in education. He writes: Today, we experience a similar lead time in respect to learning theory. The scientific study of learning began around

1890 with Wilhelm Wundt in Germany and William James in the United States. After World War II, two Americans, B. F. Skinner and Jerome Bruner, both at Harvard, developed and tested basic theories of learning. Skinner specialized in behavior and Bruner in cognition. Yet only now is learning theory beginning to become a factor in our schools." (Then follows the quote cited earlier: "Perhaps the time has come. . . ." [110]) But then Drucker makes clear that there is another difficulty that one faces with knowledge-based innovation. There is a prerequisite that must be satisfied, otherwise "knowledge-based innovation is premature and will fail." (114) To understand the prerequisite that he demands, one has to read pages 111–116 of *IE*, too long to be quoted here. But the topic of those pages is what he calls the "knowledges" that are needed for creating a knowledge-based innovation.

DRUCKER'S FIFTH IDEA— INTEGRATING SOURCES OF INNOVATION

Despite the difficulties of developing knowledge-based innovations, Drucker also writes, "Yet even the risks of high-tech innovation can be substantially reduced by integrating new knowledge as a source of innovation with one of the other sources defined earlier, the unexpected, incongruities, and especially process need." (129)

We have three additional questions based on the last three ideas just reviewed.

1. Is Drucker right, in suggesting that the time has come to build a knowledge-based innovation in education?

2. If so, how difficult would it be to plan and establish such an innovation?

3. Would it be so difficult that an appropriate comparison would be to a climb of a mountain far more difficult than Mount Everest?

Our answer to 1 as indicated above is yes, the time has come; and 2, yes, the innovation would be extraordinarily difficult *and time consuming* to establish, despite all the unexpected successes to date that one can draw on; and 3, yes the comparison to climbing a mountain more difficult than Everest is appropriate, and may even be an underestimate.*

SUMMARY OF OUR FIVE QUESTIONS

To summarize, we now give the precise form of our five questions, along with our proposed answers to them.

1. *What resources are already available in education, are seriously underutilized, and are just waiting to be endowed with a "capacity to create wealth"?*

    Students, who constitute 80 percent or more of all the people in a school, are the most promising underutilized resource.

2. *What are the changes occurring right now that provide the most promising sources for major innovations in education?*

    It is now possible to identify and produce the missing knowledges needed for a knowledge-based innovation in education. Moreover, there are enough unexpected successes and other kinds of changes occurring to make an innovation somewhat less risky than it would be if it were based only on new knowledge.

3. *Is Drucker right, in suggesting that the time has come to build a knowledge-based innovation in education?*

    Yes, the time has come.

---

* It took us a long time to appreciate just how incredibly difficult it would be to bring true reform to the entirety of U.S. schools. We had to have substantial help to come to this realization. We especially note the following books that recognized the magnitude of this task before we did: Seymour Sarason, 1990, *The Predictable Failure of Education Reform: Can We Change Course Before It Is Too Late?*, San Francisco: Jossey-Bass; and two books that form a series: Per Dalin, and Val D. Rust, *Towards Schooling for the 21st Century*, New York: Cassell; and Per Dalin, *School Development: Theories and Strategies*, New York: Cassell. Per Dalin acknowledges the profound influence on him of Matthew Miles, who recognized the challenges of education reform long ago.

4. *If so, how difficult would it be to plan and establish such an innovation?*

   Yes, the innovation would be extraordinarily difficult and time consuming to establish.

5. *Is it so difficult that an appropriate comparison would be to climbing a mountain far more difficult than Mount Everest?*

   Yes, it is appropriate and perhaps an underestimate.

THREE INITIAL DRUCKER QUESTIONS

We return to the three questions raised at the beginning.

1. Does Peter Drucker have the best ideas of anybody for how to go about reforming all of U.S. education, not just the teaching of a handful of teachers?

2. Are his best ideas included in the discussion above, or have we missed any?

3. Or if Drucker does not have the best ideas to go about reforming education, who does?

During our ten years of work based on Drucker's concept of a knowledge-based innovation, we studied close to a thousand books written from a great variety of perspectives, but we did not encounter any that came anywhere near to matching the power of Drucker's ideas for attacking the challenge of overall education reform. Nor could we find anything in Drucker's writings that would have enabled us to short-circuit the very arduous search for the needed knowledges that Drucker demanded for a knowledge-based innovation. From the perspective of what we have read or understand about education reform, we believe that Drucker has by far the best ideas for reforming all of U.S. education.

But we also know that we have far too limited knowledge of the whole education reform scene, or even of the totality of Drucker's ideas about education, to claim that our answers are more than highly tentative answers subject to change.

ASSIGNMENT AND QUESTION

The knowledge economy is critically dependent on education, and Drucker believed that our educational system is in need of revitalization and transformation. Based on this case, chapter 14 of *Management, Revised,* and any additional relevant information you can gather, identify the problems with primary and secondary education in the United States. How can education be both revitalized and transformed?

Case Number 50

What Do You Want to Be Remembered For?

When I was thirteen, I had an inspiring teacher of religion who one day went right through the class of boys asking each one, "What do you want to be remembered for?" None of us, of course, could give an answer. So, he chuckled and said, "I didn't expect you to be able to answer it. But if you still can't answer it by the time you're fifty, you will have wasted your life." We eventually had a sixtieth reunion of that high school class. Most of us were still alive, but we hadn't seen each other since we graduated, and the talk at first was a little stilted. Then one of the fellows asked, "Do you remember Father Pflieger and that question?" We remembered it. And each one said it had made all the difference to him, although they didn't really understand that until they were in their forties.

At twenty-five, some of us began to try to answer it and, by and large, answered it foolishly. Joseph Schumpeter, one of the greatest economists of this century, claimed at twenty-five that he wanted to be remembered as the best horseman in Europe, the greatest lover in Europe, and as a great economist. By age sixty, just before he died, he was asked the question again. He no longer talked about horsemanship and he no longer talked about women. He said he wanted to be remembered as the man who had given an early warning of the dangers of inflation. That is what he is to be remembered for. Asking that question changed him, even though the answer he gave at twenty-five was singularly stupid, even for a young man of twenty-five.

I'm always asking that question: What do you want to be remembered for? It is a question that induces you to renew yourself, because it pushes you to see yourself as a different person—the person you can *become.* If you are fortunate, someone with the moral authority will ask you that question early enough in your life so that you will continue to ask it as you go through life.

QUESTION

What do you want to be remembered for?